Contents

D1186738

Contents

By using *5-Minute Travel Italian* every day, you can start speaking Italian in just minutes. The 5-Minute program introduces you to a new language and gets you ready for your trip. Take a few minutes before or after work, before you go to sleep at night or any time that feels right to work on one lesson a day. If you want, you can even do some last-minute learning on the plane or train! Just have fun while you learn; you'll be speaking Italian in no time.

- The book is divided into 99 lessons. Each provides a bite-sized learning opportunity that you can complete in minutes.

- Each unit has 8 lessons presenting important vocabulary, phrases and other information needed while you travel.

- A review at the end of each unit provides an opportunity to test your knowledge before you move on.

- Unless otherwise noted, *5-Minute Travel Italian* uses formal language. In everyday Italian, the formal is usually used between adults who are not close friends or family and in professional settings. The informal is used with friends and family and when addressing children.

Buongiorno!

- Real life language and activities introduce the vocabulary, phrases and grammar covered in the lessons that follow. You'll see dialogues, postcards, e-mails and other everyday correspondence in Italian.

- You can listen to the dialogues, articles, e-mails and other presentations on the *5-Minute Travel Italian* audio CD.

5-Minute Travel Italian audio
When you see this symbol , you'll know to listen to the specified track on the *5-Minute Travel Italian* audio CD.

Smart Phrases

- In these lessons you'll find useful everyday phrases. You can listen to these phrases on the audio program.

- Extra Phrases enrich your knowledge and understanding of everyday Italian. These are not practiced in the activities, but they're there for those who want to learn.

SMART TIP

Boxes like these are here to extend your Italian knowledge. You'll find extra language conventions and other helpful information on how to speak Italian.

Words to Know

- Core Words are important words related to the lesson topic. In some lessons these words are divided into sub-categories. You can listen to these words on our audio program.

- Extra Words are other helpful words to know.

CULTURE TIP

Boxes like these introduce useful cultural information about Italy.

Smart Grammar

- Don't let the name scare you. Smart Grammar covers the basic parts of speech you'll need to know if you want to speak Italian easily and fluently.

- From verb usage to forming questions, the 5-Minute program provides quick and easy explanations and examples for how to use these structures.

Unit Review Here you'll have a chance to practice what you've learned.

Challenge
Extend your knowledge even further with a challenge activity.

Internet Activity

SMART PRONUNCIATION

Boxes like these demonstrate specific pronunciation tools. For example, did you know that the pronunciation of the letters *c* and *g* vary based on which vowel follows them? You'll learn more as you move further along in the book.

- Internet activities take you to **www.berlitzbooks.com/5Mtravel**, where you can test drive your new language skills. Just look for the computer symbol.

This section is designed to make you familiar with the sounds of Italian using our simplified phonetic transcription. You'll find the pronunciation of the Italian letters and sounds explained below, together with their "imitated" equivalents. Simply read the pronunciation as if it were English, noting any special rules below.

The accents ´ and ` indicate stress, e.g. *città*, cheet-<u>tah</u>. Some Italian words have more than one meaning. In these instances, the accent mark is also used to distinguish between them, e.g.: *è* (is) and *e* (and); *dà* (gives) and *da* (from).

Remember that all letters, with the exception of *h*, are sounded: this includes final vowels in words like *passaporto*, *mangiare* etc. Note also that double consonants are distinctly pronounced by holding (or lengthening) the sound.

Consonants

Letter	Approximate Pronunciation	Example	Pronunciation
c	1. before e and i soft sound like ch in chip	**cerco**	<u>chehr</u>·koh
	2. before a, o, u hard sound like c in cat	**conto**	<u>kohn</u>·toh
ch	always hard sound like in cat	**che**	keh
g	1. before e and i, like j in jet	**valigia**	vah·<u>lee</u>·jyah
	2. before a, o, u, like g in get	**pagare**	pah·<u>gah</u>·reh
gg	pronounced more intensely	**viaggio**	<u>vyah</u>·djoh
gh	always hard sound like g in go	**spaghetti**	spah·<u>gheht</u>·tee
gli	like lli in million	**bagaglio**	bah·<u>gah</u>·llyoh
gn	like the first n in onion	**bagno**	<u>bah</u>·nyoh
h	always silent	**ho**	oh
r	rolled at the back of the mouth	**Roma**	<u>roh</u>·mah
s	1. like s in same	**sole**	soh·leh
	2. sometimes, between two vowels, like z in zoo	**rosa**	roh·zah
sc	1. before e and i, like sh in shut	**uscita**	oo·shee·tah
	2. before a, o, u, like sk in skin	**scarpa**	skahr·pah
z/zz	1. generally like ts in hits	**grazie**	grah·tsyeh
	2. sometimes a little softer like dz in zebra	**zero**	dzeh·roh

Letters b, d, f, l, m, n, p, q, t, v are pronounced as in English. The letters j, k, w, x and y are used in foreign origin words.

Vowels

Letter	Approximate Pronunciation	Example	Pronunciation
a	like a in father	**pagare**	pah·<u>gah</u>·reh
e	1. like e in get	**destra**	<u>deh</u>·strah
	2. before a single consonant, sometimes like e in they	**sete**	<u>say</u>·teh
i	like ee in meet	**sì**	see
o	1. like o in soft	**notte**	<u>noht</u>·teh
	2. like o in cold	**sole**	<u>soh</u>·leh
u	like oo in food	**uno**	<u>oo</u>·noh

Vowel Combinations

ae	paese	pah·<u>eh</u>·zeh
ao	Paolo	<u>pah</u>·oh·loh
au	auto	<u>ow</u>·toh
eo	museo	moo·<u>zeh</u>·oh
eu	euro	<u>eh</u>·oo·roh
ei	lei	lay
ia	piazza	<u>pyah</u>·tsah
ie	chiesa	<u>kyeh</u>·zah
io	stazione	stah-<u>tsyoh</u>-neh
iu	più	pyoo
ua	quale	<u>kwah</u>·leh
ue	questo	<u>kweh</u>·stoh
ui	qui	kwee
uo	può	pwoh

Unit 1   Preparing for Travel

In this unit you will learn:
- **how to talk about different means of transportation.**
- **personal pronouns and the verb *andare* (to go).**
- **the days of the week and the months of the year.**
- **how to check in at the airport.**

LESSON 1

Buon viaggio!

Dialogue

Mr. Conti is talking to his colleague, Mrs. Nepi, who is getting ready to go on a trip.

Il sig. Conti	Dove va in vacanza?
La sig.ra Nepi	Vado a Napoli.
Il sig. Conti	Va in aereo?
La sig.ra Nepi	No, prendo il treno.

SMART TIPS

- Did you notice that Italian often doesn't use the subject in a sentence? Instead of saying *Io vado a Napoli*, you can say *Vado a Napoli*.

- *Sig.* is the abbreviation for *signore*, "Mr." *Sig.ra* is the abbreviation for *signora*, "Mrs." *Sig.na* is the abbreviation for *signorina*, "Miss." The abbreviations are not capitalized when they're followed by the last name (*la sig.ra Ansemi, il sig. Biondi*).

Activity A

Circle **T** for true and **F** for false.

1   La sig.ra Nepi is going on a business trip.   **T / F**
2   La sig.ra Nepi is going to Naples.   **T / F**
3   La sig.ra Nepi is going by plane.   **T / F**
4   La sig.ra Nepi is going by train.   **T / F**

Activity B

Listen to the dialogue again and fill in the missing words.

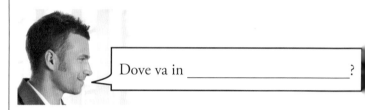

Dove va in _____?

_____ a Napoli.

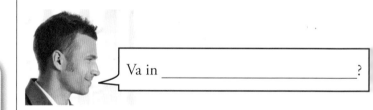

Va in _____?

No, prendo il _____.

CULTURE TIP

Did you know that the average Italian worker gets between 20 and 30 days of paid vacation a year?

Core Words

  l'aereo   airplane (m)

  l'auto   car

  l'autobus   bus

  la bicicletta bicycle

  la crociera   cruise

  la metro   subway

  la navetta   shuttle

  il taxi   taxi

  il traghetto   ferry

         il treno   train

Activity A

Match the picture in the left column with the correct Italian word in the right column.

1    a l'aereo

2    b la bicicletta

3   c il traghetto

4    d l'auto

5   e la metro

Activity B

Use the words below to identify the best means of travel for each example.

> l'aereo   l'auto   la bicicletta   la navetta   il traghetto

1 traveling from New
   York to Naples   _____

2 taking a guided tour
   down the Tiber River   _____

3 getting from the airport
   to your hotel   _____

4 driving through the
   Po River valley   _____

5 pedaling through
   the center of Florence _____

Smart Phrases

Core Phrases

Prende il traghetto.	She is taking a ferry.
Andiamo in aereo.	We are going by plane.
In Italia noleggio un'auto.	In Italy I am going to rent a car.
Andate in crociera.	You are going on a cruise.
Dov'è il parcheggio dei taxi?	Where is the taxi stand [taxi rank]?
C'è un servizio di navetta?	Is there shuttle service?
Deve prendere la metro.	You must take the subway.
Noleggia una bicicletta.	He is going to rent a bicycle.

SMART TIP

You may have noticed some different articles in these examples. *Il* (m)/*la* (f) are definite articles and *un* (m)/*una* (f)/*un'* (f) are indefinite articles. For example, *l'auto* is "<u>the</u> car" while *un'auto* is "<u>a</u> car."

CULTURE TIP

If you decide to rent a car in Europe, sometimes bigger isn't always better. A smaller car will allow you to easily navigate the narrow roads of some of the larger cities and will also make parking a lot easier! Be careful, though, because most rental cars in Europe are standard, not automatic. If you need an automatic, make sure you request one ahead of time.

Activity A

Fill in the blank using the image as a guide.

1 Andate in _____.

2 Dov'è il parcheggio dei _____?

3 In Italia noleggio un' _____.

4 Andiamo in _____.

Activity B

How would you…

1 …ask where the taxi stand is?

_____

2 …tell someone you're going to rent a car?

_____

3 …say that she is taking a ferry?

_____

4 …ask if there is shuttle service?

_____

Smart Grammar

Personal Pronouns

io	I
tu	you (sing., inf.)
Lei	you (sing., form.)
lui/lei	he/she
noi	we
voi	you (pl., form. and inf.)
loro	they

Abbreviations

masculine	m	singular	sing.	informal	inf.
feminine	f	plural	pl.	formal	form.

SMART TIP

It is important to distinguish between the formal and informal pronouns in Italian. When speaking to friends, colleagues you're familiar with, children and pets, use the informal *tu*. However, when talking to strangers or someone that you've just met, it is preferable to use the formal *Lei* until the other person says that you can use the informal *tu*.

Activity A

Write the correct singular pronoun under each picture.

1 (I) _____ vado in vacanza.

2 (He) _____ va a Napoli.

3 (She) _____ va a Roma.

4 (You, form.) _____ va a Milano.

Activity B

Fill in the blanks with the correct plural personal pronoun.

1 (We) _____ andiamo in auto.

2 (They) _____ vanno in aereo.

3 (You, pl.) _____ andate in treno.

4 (They) _____ vanno in crociera.

SMART TIPS

- You may have noticed that there isn't an Italian equivalent of "it." Italian does have one but it's hardly ever used. If you want to say, "It's big," referring to a car, just say *È grande*. The same for plural: "They are small" (referring to cars) is *Sono piccole*.

- The English personal pronoun "you" has a few different translations in Italian. It can be *tu* (sing. inf.), *Lei* (sing. form., always capitalized) or *voi* (pl., both form. and inf.). The word *lei*, without capitalization, also means "she."

The Departure

Robert is planning a trip to Italy. Here's a list of what he needs to do before he goes.

DA FARE

fare il biglietto	buy my ticket
rinnovare il passaporto	renew my passport
fare le valigie	pack my bags
scegliere una guida	choose a guide book
cambiare i dollari/ le sterline in euro	change dollars/ pounds into euros
trovare un albergo	find a hotel
prenotare un'auto a noleggio	reserve a rental car
imparare meglio l'italiano	learn more Italian

SMART TIPS

- Why is *il, la* or *l'* (the) used in the examples above, and not a possessive adjective (my)? When the context makes it clear who owns something, the possessive isn't used.

- All of the verbs above are in the infinitive, the most basic form of a verb. In later lessons you will learn how to conjugate the three main groups of Italian verbs, *-are, -ere* and *-ire* verbs, as well as irregular verbs.

Activity A

Fill in the missing words.

1 fare il _____

2 fare le _____

3 cambiare i _____ / le _____ in _____

4 rinnovare il _____

5 prenotare un'_____ a noleggio

Activity B

Are you going on vacation soon? Make a list of some things you need to do before you go!

DA FARE

1. _____
2. _____
3. _____
4. _____
5. _____

LESSON 6

Words to Know

SETTEMBRE

VIAGGIO

Core Words

I giorni della settimana
(Days of the Week)

lunedì	Monday
martedì	Tuesday
mercoledì	Wednesday
giovedì	Thursday
venerdì	Friday
sabato	Saturday
domenica	Sunday

I mesi dell'anno
(Months of the Year)

gennaio	January
febbraio	February
marzo	March
aprile	April
maggio	May
giugno	June
luglio	July
agosto	August
settembre	September
ottobre	October
novembre	November
dicembre	December

Extra Words

oggi	today
domani	tomorrow
ieri	yesterday
il giorno	day
la settimana	week
il mese	month
l'anno	year

CULTURE TIP

While the week begins with Sunday on American calendars, it begins with Monday on Italian calendars. Be especially careful if you're booking reservations online.

Activity A

Label the following numbered days of the week.

Febbraio

L	M	M	G	V	S	D
	1.			2.		
3.					4.	
		5.				6.
			7.			

1 _____   5 _____

2 _____   6 _____

3 _____   7 _____

4 _____

Activity B

Put the months in order from 1–12.

agosto	_____	marzo	_____
dicembre	_____	febbraio	_____
aprile	_____	ottobre	_____
novembre	_____	maggio	_____
luglio	_____	giugno	_____
gennaio	_____	settembre	_____

SMART TIPS

- Days and months begin with lower-case letters in Italian, unlike their upper-case equivalents in English. You often find capitalized months in calendars.

- In Italy, dates are abbreviated in the order day/month/year. For example, January 8, 2011 would be 8.1.2011. August 1, 2011 would be 1.8.2011.

LESSON 7

Smart Phrases

Core Phrases

check-in online	online check-in
le Sue prenotazioni	your current reservations
stampi la Sua carta d'imbarco	print your boarding pass
orari dei voli in tempo reale	real-time flight status
numero di prenotazione	reservation number
scelga il posto	choose your seat
modifichi la data e l'orario del volo	modify the date and time of your flight

Activity A

Jane has decided to check in for her flight online. Use the words from the word bank to tell her where she needs to click in order to…

> numero di prenotazione
> stampi la Sua carta d'imbarco
> check-in online

1   …begin checking in online.

_____

2   …enter her reservation number.

_____

3   …print her boarding pass.

_____

Activity B

Match the following links to their English equivalents.

1   scelga il posto

2   orari dei voli in tempo reale

3   le Sue prenotazioni

4   check-in online

a online check-in   **c** your current reservations

b choose your seat   **d** real-time flight status

Activity C

Put the following steps in order to check in and print your boarding pass.

____ Click on *scelga il posto.*

____ Click on *check-in online.*

____ Enter your *numero di prenotazione.*

____ Click on *stampi la Sua carta d'imbarco.*

Activity D

What should Jane click on if she wants to…

1   …change the date of her flight?

_____

2   …change her seat?

_____

3   …make sure her flight is on time?

_____

The verb *andare* (to go)

The verb *andare* is irregular. The chart shows its conjugation in the present tense.

(io)	vado	I go
(tu)	vai	you go
(Lei)	va	you go
(lui/lei)	va	he/she goes
(noi)	andiamo	we go
(voi)	andate	you go
(loro)	vanno	they go

SMART TIP

The verb *andare* is often before an infinitive to express the idea of going someplace to do something. *Vado a mangiare*, "I'm going to eat," means that you're going somewhere (to the kitchen, to the restaurant, etc.) to eat.

Activity A

Fill in the blank with the correct form of *andare*.

1 (noi) _____ in Italia.

2 (Lei) _____ in vacanza.

3 (io) _____ all'aeroporto.

4 (loro) _____ a Pisa in treno.

5 (voi) _____ a Roma.

6 (tu) _____ all'aeroporto.

7 (lui) _____ a fare il biglietto.

8 (loro) _____ in crociera.

Activity B

Answer the following questions using *sì*, "yes."

Example: Vai a Roma?
Sì, vado a Roma.

1 Andiamo a Genova?

_____

2 Andate a Bologna?

_____

3 Vanno a Cagliari?

_____

4 Vai a Venezia?

_____

SMART TIP

Some questions can be formed in Italian without making any changes to the sentence; just change your intonation. If your voice goes up at the end, it's a question! For example:

(Lei) Va a Roma.   You go to Rome.

(Lei) Va a Roma?   Are you going to Rome?

Activity C

Complete the following sentences with the correct form of *andare*.

 1 (noi) _____ a Pisa.

 2 (Lei) _____ a Parigi.

 3 (io) _____ a Londra.

 4 (loro) _____ a Barcellona.

 5 (tu) _____ a New York.

Unit 1   Review

Activity A

Label the following means of transportation.

1 _____

2 _____

3 _____

4 _____

Activity B

Listen to the dialogue from Lesson 1 and fill in the blanks below.

Il sig. Conti	Dove _____ in vacanza?
La sig.ra Nepi	_____ a Napoli.
Il sig. Conti	Va _____?
La sig.ra Nepi	No, prendo _____.

Activity C

Put the days of the week in order from 1–7.

___ mercoledì
___ domenica
___ lunedì
___ giovedì
___ sabato
___ martedì
___ venerdì

Activity D

Complete the following table for the verb *andare*.

io	
	vai
Lei	
lui/lei	
noi	
	andate
	vanno

Activity E

Complete the word search to find words related to travel, days and months.

aereo	auto	crociera
domenica	gennaio	lei
noi	sabato	traghetto
vacanza	vado	valigie

```
T  R  A  G  H  E  T  T  O  C  I  L  Q  S
Q  N  W  R  D  Z  T  R  A  Z  T  Y  P  A
L  D  S  C  V  Q  L  I  P  B  N  G  O  B
V  A  L  I  G  I  E  W  R  K  Z  E  V  A
T  U  M  O  P  Y  I  D  Y  M  E  N  E  T
C  T  P  D  C  A  Z  R  C  V  J  N  Y  O
Z  O  X  F  E  V  A  C  A  N  Z  A  R  C
V  X  Q  T  U  P  E  P  N  M  K  I  L  P
V  B  E  N  C  R  R  T  Y  C  V  O  N  L
A  K  T  O  M  R  E  W  R  V  B  N  M  T
D  Q  F  I  G  D  O  M  E  N  I  C  A  I
O  T  V  N  T  R  S  Q  H  A  W  A  T  P
R  C  R  O  C  I  E  R  A  R  E  W  R  T
T  Q  S  Z  D  R  T  U  I  P  Y  O  P  E
```

Internet Activity

Want help practicing your verb conjugations? Go to iTunes® and search for "Berlitz" to download the Berlitz verb app for your iPod touch® or iPhone®. The more you practice your verbs, the easier they become!

In this unit you will learn:
- the numbers 0–60 and time.
- how to greet others and introduce yourself.
- the verb *essere* (to be).
- how to talk about different countries, languages and nationalities.

LESSON 1

Mi chiamo…

Dialogue

Catherine has just boarded her plane to Italy and the gentleman seated next to her decides to strike up a conversation.

Giorgio	Buongiorno. Mi chiamo Giorgio Laghi. Lei come si chiama?
Catherine	Buongiorno. Mi chiamo Catherine Dover. Piacere.
Giorgio	Piacere. È americana?
Catherine	Sì, sono americana. E Lei è italiano?
Giorgio	No, sono svizzero. È in vacanza?
Catherine	Sì, sono in vacanza. Vado a Roma.

SMART TIPS

- A very easy way to say "Nice to meet you" in Italian is *piacere*.
- Check the Italian-English glossary on page 115 to find out how to say other nationalities.

Activity A

Circle **T** for true and **F** for false.

1	Giorgio asks Catherine what her name is.	T / F
2	Catherine is happy to meet Giorgio.	T / F
3	Catherine is Italian.	T / F
4	Giorgio is on vacation.	T / F

Activity B

Imagine you are seated next to Giorgio. How would you respond?

Buongiorno. Mi chiamo Giorgio Laghi. Lei come si chiama?

Lei _____

Piacere. È americana/o?

Lei _____

Sì, sono italiano. È in vacanza?

Lei _____

CULTURE TIPS

- When you meet someone in Italy, it is customary to shake hands. If you're meeting a friend or family member, though, it is customary to *dare due baci*, or "give two kisses."
- Did you know? Italian is one of the official languages in Switzerland, together with German and French.

LESSON 2
Words to Know

Core Words

I numeri (Numbers)

zero	0	tredici	13
uno	1	quattordici	14
due	2	quindici	15
tre	3	sedici	16
quattro	4	diciassette	17
cinque	5	diciotto	18
sei	6	diciannove	19
sette	7	venti	20
otto	8	ventuno	21
nove	9	trenta	30
dieci	10	quaranta	40
undici	11	cinquanta	50
dodici	12	sessanta	60

Extra Words

l'indirizzo	address
il numero di telefono	phone number
il numero del volo	flight number

Activity A

How many of each do you see?

1  _____ biglietti

2  _____ valigie

3 _____ turisti

4  _____ taxi

SMART TIP

The number 1 can be either masculine or feminine in Italian depending on the gender of the noun. For example, *un biglietto* (m) is "one ticket" and *una valigia* (f) is "one suitcase."

Activity B

Look at the flight departure screen and say what time the following flights are scheduled to leave.

PARTENZE			
13.40	ROMA	AT 0026	IN ORARIO
13.55	AMSTERDAM	KL 2215	IN ORARIO
14.05	MILANO	AT 6509	RITARDO 30 MIN
14.15	BERLINO	LH 1550	IN ORARIO
14.30	LONDRA	BA 3022	IN ORARIO
14.40	MADRID	IB 0045	IN ORARIO

1 zero zero quarantacinque _____

2 sessantacinque zero nove _____

3 trenta ventidue _____

4 ventidue quindici _____

Activity C

Listen to the phone numbers and write them down.

1 _____

2 _____

3 _____

SMART TIP

If the number that follows *venti, trenta* etc., begins with a vowel, that vowel is dropped. For example, *venti* and *uno* become *ventuno* (21). All numbers ending with *tre* (3) have an accent mark: *ottantatré* (83).

Smart Phrases

Core Phrases

Salve.	Hello.
Buongiorno.	Good morning.
Buonasera.	Good evening.
Buonanotte.	Good night.
Come si chiama?	What's your name?
Mi chiamo ____.	My name is ____.
Come sta?	How are you?
Bene, grazie.	I'm fine, thanks.
Di dov'è?	Where are you from?
Arrivederci.	Goodbye.

Extra Phrases

Ciao!	Hi!
Tutto bene?	How's it going?
Tutto bene.	I'm fine.
A presto!	See you soon!

SMART TIPS

- Remember that there are different levels of formality in Italian. For example, you would say *Ciao, come va?* to a friend, but *Buongiorno, come sta?* to a stranger.

- *Buongiorno* literally means "good day," but it's used the same as "Good morning" in English.

Activity A

Answer the following questions.

1 Come sta?

_____

2 Come si chiama?

_____

3 Di dov'è?

_____

Activity B

What would these people say to each other?

1

2

3

4

LESSON 4
Smart Grammar

The verb *essere* (to be)

The verb *essere* is irregular. The chart shows its conjugation in the present tense.

(io)	sono	I am
(tu)	sei	you are
(Lei)	è	you are
(lui/lei)	è	he/she is
(noi)	siamo	we are
(voi)	siete	you are
(loro)	sono	they are

SMART TIP

Now that you know the verb *essere*, two good expressions to learn are *c'è*, which means "there is" and *ci sono*, which means "there are." For example, *C'è un volo per Pisa*, "There is a flight to Pisa." Likewise, *Ci sono due treni per Firenze* means "There are two trains to Florence."

Activity A
Fill in the blanks with the correct form of the verb *essere*.

1 Catherine _____ americana.

2 Fabrizio e Giorgio non _____ francesi.

3 (noi) _____ in vacanza.

4 (loro) _____ in aereo.

SMART TIP

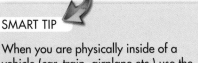

When you are physically inside of a vehicle (car, train, airplane etc.) use the preposition *in* (in) in Italian. For example, *Sono in auto* means "I am in the car." The same preposition is used with the verb *andare* (to go) to express "to go by...." *Vado a Roma in aereo* means "I'm going to Rome by plane."

Activity B
Answer the following questions in the affirmative.

1 È in vacanza?

_____

2 Giorgio Laghi è italiano?

_____

3 Catherine e Julie sono americane?

_____

4 Sono in treno?

_____

5 Sei in taxi?

_____

Activity C
Complete the verb chart with the present form of *essere*.

io	
tu	
Lei	
lui/lei	
noi	
voi	
loro	

Your Turn
Do you know any adjectives in Italian that would complete the statement? Use a bilingual dictionary or the glossary for help.

Sono _____.

A che ora è il treno?

ROMA TERMINI

Partenze	Arrivi		
ORARIO	DESTINAZIONE	TRENO	BINARIO
19:25	BOLOGNA	8477	3
19:30	TORINO	8375	6
19:34	NAPOLI	16761	--
19:35	MILANO	8761	--
19:50	BOLOGNA	8479	--

Activity A

Listen to the questions and answer them based on the train schedule at left.

1 _____

2 _____

3 _____

4 _____

CULTURE TIP

The Italians use a 24-hour clock, so there is no AM or PM, even though the hours from 12 to 24 are used only in official timetables. In everyday language, you can usually understand from the context whether morning or afternoon is meant. If it is necessary, add *di mattina* (in the morning), *di pomeriggio* (in the afternoon), *di sera* (in the evening) and *di notte* (at night). For example: *Sono le otto di mattina,* "It's 8 a.m."

SMART TIPS

- "A quarter after," is *e un quarto*. For example, *6.15* is *le sei e un quarto*.
- "A quarter to," is *meno un quarto*. For example, *7.45* is, *le otto meno un quarto*.
- "Half past," is *e mezzo*. For example, *8.30* is *le otto e mezzo*.
- Noon is *mezzogiorno* and midnight is *mezzanotte*.

Dialogue

Now that you know numbers, let's talk about time. Listen to the conversation between Stephanie and the train conductor.

Mi scusi. A che ora è il prossimo treno per Bologna?

Il prossimo treno è alle diciannove e venticinque.

E il treno successivo?

Il treno successivo è alle diciannove e quaranta.

SMART TIP

Il prossimo treno means "the next train," while *il treno successivo* means "the following train."

Activity B

Listen to the times said by the conductor and write which train leaves at each time.

1 _____

2 _____

3 _____

4 _____

MILANO CENTRALE

Partenze	Arrivi		
ORARIO	DESTINAZIONE	TRENO	BINARIO
18:25	ROMA	3127	19
18:30	COMO	13119	22
18:33	FIRENZE	850053	--
18:45	BOLZANO	3353	--
18:50	REGGIO CALABRIA	3131	--

Core Words

Bandiera (Flag)	Paese (Country)	Nazionalità (Nationality)	Lingua (Language)
	L'Australia	australiano/australiana (m/f)	l'inglese
	La Francia	francese (m/f)	il francese
	La Germania	tedesco/tedesca (m/f)	il tedesco
	L'Inghilterra	inglese (m/f)	l'inglese
	L'Italia	italiano/italiana (m/f)	l'italiano
	La Spagna	spagnolo/spagnola (m/f)	lo spagnolo
	Gli Stati Uniti	americano/americana (m/f)	l'inglese

SMART TIP

Note that *la nazionalità*, the nationality, and *la lingua*, the language, aren't capitalized in Italian like they are in English. For example:

Lui è italiano.   He is Italian.
Io parlo italiano.   I speak Italian.

Activity A
Match each country with its flag.

1 Gli Stati Uniti   a
2 L'Italia   b
3 L'Inghilterra   c
4 La Spagna   d
5 La Francia   e
6 La Germania   f

SMART TIP

Check page 115 in the glossary to learn more countries and nationalities.

Activity B
Write the language associated with each country below. Remember not to capitalize it!

1 La Francia _____

2 La Germania _____

3 Gli Stati Uniti _____

4 L'Italia _____

Activity C
Listen to the sentences describing the people below and label them from 1–4.

_____

_____

Smart Phrases

Why Travel?

Siamo in vacanza.	We are on vacation.
Sono in viaggio di lavoro.	I am on a business trip.
Va a trovare la famiglia.	He is going to visit his family.
Andate a fare un'escursione in Sicilia.	You are going hiking in Sicily.
Vanno a sciare sulle Alpi.	They are going skiing in the Alps.
Vai a Roma a studiare italiano.	You are going to Rome to study Italian.
Va a fare surf in Sardegna.	She is going surfing in Sardinia.

Activity A

Number the following travel ideas from 1–5 where 1 is your favorite and 5 is your least favorite.

_____ fare un viaggio di lavoro

_____ andare a sciare sulle Alpi

_____ andare a studiare italiano a Roma

_____ andare a trovare la famiglia

_____ andare a fare un'escursione in Sicilia

Activity B

Say why the following people are travelling.

1 _____

2 _____

3 _____

4 _____

5 _____

SMART TIP

In Italian, you use the verb *visitare* to talk about visiting places and monuments. You use the expression *andare a trovare* to talk about visiting people. For example, *Visito il Colosseo*, "I visit the Colosseum," and *Vado a trovare la mia famiglia*, "I visit my family."

LESSON 8

Smart Grammar

Masculine and Feminine

As you learned in Unit 1, all nouns have a gender in Italian. Here are some hints to help you identify the genders of different nouns.

- Almost all words that end in –o are masculine. For example:

l'aereo	plane
il traghetto	ferry
il piano	floor
il viaggio	trip

- The word *auto* (car) ends in –o and is feminine. Why? Because it's short for *automobile* (f). The same is true for *la metro* (subway), which is short for *metropolitana* (f).

- Almost all words that end in –a are feminine. For example:

la borsa	bag
la domanda	question
la navetta	shuttle
la valigia	suitcase

- Words that end in –e can be either masculine or feminine. For example:

l'inglese	English language (m)
l'escursione	hike (f)

SMART TIPS

- To say that you are going to a country, use the preposition *in*.

  Vado in Italia. (I'm going to Italy).
  Va in Giappone. (He's going to Japan).

- Use the preposition *a* for cities.

  Va a Roma. (She's going to Rome).
  Andiamo a Berlino. (We're going to Berlin).

Activity A

Identify the following nouns. Don't forget to put the definite article!

1 _____

2 _____

3 _____

4 _____

SMART TIPS

- When forming the plural in Italian, the last letter of the word changes. In general, –o > –i, –a > –e, and –e > –i. For example: *battello/battelli, valigia/valigie, escursione/escursioni*.

- Most masculine plural nouns take the definite article *i*: *i castelli* (the castles). *Gli* is used with masculine nouns that begin with a vowel or s + consonant, z– or gn–: *gli aerei* (the planes), *gli Stati Uniti* (the United States). *Le* is used with feminine plural nouns: *le biciclette* (the bicycles).

- The words *auto, metro* and *taxi* don't change in the plural, but they do take the plural article: *le auto, le metro, i taxi*.

Activity B

Insert the correct preposition (*a* or *in*).

1 Giulia va _____ Venezia.

2 Cristina e Silvano vanno _____ Spagna.

3 Marisa va _____ Svizzera (Switzerland).

4 Vai _____ Marocco (Morocco).

5 Andiamo _____ Firenze.

Review

Activity A

Circle the highest number in each group.

sessantadue	due	diciassette
cinquantatré	cinque	diciannove
diciannove	undici	sedici

Activity B

Say the nationality and language spoken by the following people.

1 Sono _____

   e parlo _____ .

2 Sono _____

   e parlo _____ .

3 Sono _____

   e parlo _____ .

Activity C

Practice saying the following phone numbers out loud.

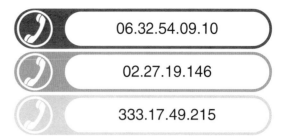

06.32.54.09.10

02.27.19.146

333.17.49.215

Activity D

See if you can understand when the next train leaves.

Il prossimo treno parte alle…

1 _____   3 _____

2 _____   4 _____

Activity E

Write the definite article *il*, *la* or *l'* before each noun.

1 _____   traghetto
2 _____   auto
3 _____   lingua
4 _____   passaporto
5 _____   inglese

> ### Challenge
> List five different countries along with their nationalities and the languages spoken.

Internet Activity

Go to **www.berlitzbooks.com/5Mtravel** to find a link to a site where you can practice reserving a train ticket. The box labeled BIGLIETTI is dedicated to reservations.

In this unit you will learn:
- how to find your way through the airport and go through customs.
- the verb *avere* (to have).
- how to get from the airport to your hotel.
- how to navigate public transportation.

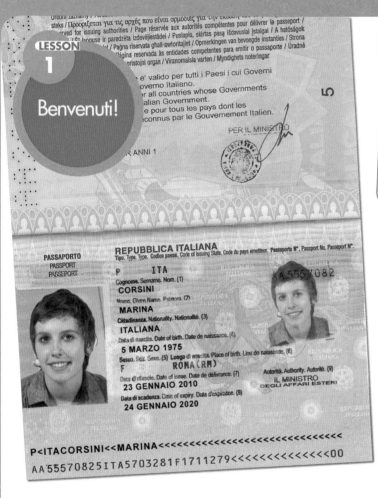

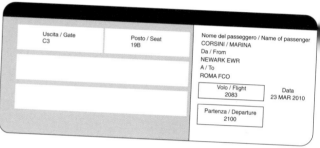

Marina was in the United States for vacation and is on her way back to Rome. Here are her passport and ticket.

Activity A

The airline seems to have misplaced one of Marina's suitcases. Help her fill out the following Lost Luggage form using the information from her passport and ticket stub.

MODULO DI SEGNALAZIONE PER SMARRIMENTO BAGAGLIO

Cognome: _____

Nome: _____

Cittadinanza: _____

Data di nascita: _____

Data del volo: _____

Volo: _____

SMART TIP

Italians use the metric system. The measure of height used in a passport is the centimeter: 2.5cm is approximately one inch.

Activity B

Match the Italian word to the English word.

1 cognome   a first name
2 data di nascita   b last name
3 nome   c gate
4 luogo di nascita   d date of birth
5 uscita   e place of birth

Words to Know

Core Words

gli arrivi	arrivals
il controllo passaporti	passport control
il dazio doganale	customs duty
dichiarare	to declare
la dogana	customs
gli effetti personali	personal belongings
il passaporto	passport
il ritiro bagagli	baggage claim
il terminal	terminal
i trasporti pubblici	public transportation
l'uscita	exit
il visto	visa

Extra Words

il carrello	baggage cart
la guardia di finanza	customs officer
lo scalo	stopover

Activity A

Listen to the words and numbers on the CD and label the following images 1–5.

_____   _____   _____

_____   _____

Activity B

Imagine that you just arrived at the airport. Label the following steps from 1–5, where 1 is the first thing you have to do.

_____ passare la dogana

_____ arrivare al terminal

_____ trovare l'uscita

_____ andare al ritiro bagagli

_____ passare il controllo passaporti

SMART TIP

Did you notice that it also said *uscita* on Marina's ticket? *Uscita* can mean both "exit" and "gate."

Activity C

Read the clues and complete the crossword puzzle.

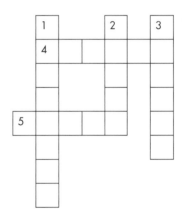

Across

4 not departures

5 you take it to fly

Down

1 you take it to carry your luggage

2 you need it to enter some countries

3 you go there to get your luggage

LESSON 3

Smart Phrases

Core Phrases

Ha qualcosa da dichiarare?	Do you have anything to declare?
Non ho niente da dichiarare.	I have nothing to declare.
Quanto tempo rimane in Italia?	How long will you stay in Italy?
Rimango due giorni/settimane.	I'm going to stay for two days/weeks.
Motivo del viaggio?	What is the purpose of your trip?
Sono in vacanza/in viaggio di lavoro.	I am on vacation/business.

Extra Phrases

Sono in transito.	I am just passing through.
Voglio dichiarare due bottiglie di spumante.	I want to declare two bottles of sparkling wine.
Apra questa valigia, per favore.	Please open this suitcase.

SMART TIP

In order to say "this/these" in Italian, you use the words *questo/questa* (m/f) for singular and *questi/queste* (m/f) for plural. For example, "this ticket" is *questo biglietto* and "these bags" is *queste borse*.

Activity A

Choose the best answer for each question.

1   Ha qualcosa da dichiarare?
    a **No, sono in viaggio di lavoro.**
    b **No, non ho niente da dichiarare.**

2   Quanto tempo rimane in Italia?
    a **Rimango due settimane.**
    b **Sono due ore.**

3   Motivo del viaggio?
    a **Vado a trovare la mia famiglia.**
    b **Sono svizzero.**

4   Non ha niente da dichiarare?
    a **Sì, sono in vacanza.**
    b **Sì, voglio dichiarare quattro bottiglie di cognac.**

Activity B

Insert the correct demonstrative pronoun (*questo, questa, questi* or *queste*) below.

1   _____ aereo

2   _____ uomini

3   _____ navetta

4   _____ valigie

Smart Grammar

The verb *avere* (to have)

The verb *avere* is irregular. The chart shows its conjugation in the present tense.

(io)	ho	I have
(tu)	hai	you have
(Lei)	ha	you have
(lui/lei)	ha	he/she has
(noi)	abbiamo	we have
(voi)	avete	you have
(loro)	hanno	they have

SMART TIP

Did you notice something special in four of the forms of *avere*? *Ho, hai, ha* and *hanno* are the first Italian words beginning with "h" you've seen—in fact, they are the only ones! (*Hotel* starts with "h" too, but it is not an Italian word). Don't pronounce the "h"—it's always silent.

Activity A

Fill in the blanks with the correct form of *avere*.

1   (noi) _____ un'auto a noleggio.

2   (io) _____ due valigie.

3   Giacomo _____ un passaporto italiano.

4   Rachele e Anna _____ un biglietto di andata e ritorno.

Activity B

Complete the verb table for the verb *avere*.

io	
tu	
Lei	
lui/lei	
noi	
voi	
loro	

SMART TIP

The verb *avere* can be used to express a variety of feelings in Italian.

Examples

Ho sete.	I'm thirsty.
Ha fame.	He's hungry.
Abbiamo paura.	We're afraid.
Hanno sonno.	They're sleepy.
Hai freddo.	You're cold.
Hanno caldo.	They're hot.

Activity C

Listen to the audio and match each statement with the correct picture.

1   _____   2   _____

3   _____   4   _____

5   _____

Taxi!

Dialogue

Frank has just arrived in Rome and is taking a taxi to his hotel. Follow along with the dialogue while listening to the audio.

Tassista Dove andate?

Frank Buongiorno. Andiamo all'Hotel Mercurio.

Tassista Sa l'indirizzo?

Frank Via Fontana 25. Posso pagare con la carta di credito?

Tassista Mi dispiace ma posso accettare soltanto contanti.

Frank Mi può dare la ricevuta, per favore?

Activity A

What really happened to Frank? Circle **T** for True and **F** for False.

1   Frank prende l'autobus.   **T / F**
2   Frank va all'Hotel Mercurio.   **T / F**
3   Può pagare con la carta di credito.   **T / F**
4   Frank vuole la ricevuta.   **T / F**

SMART TIP

There are a few different ways of saying "receipt" in Italian. For example, in a taxi, you ask for *la ricevuta*, at a hotel and in a restaurant you ask for *la fattura*, and at a store, you ask for *lo scontrino*. Make sure that you never leave a restaurant, bar or shop without your receipt because the police could check and the customer is required to keep it.

Activity B

Pretend you are Frank and answer the taxi driver's questions.

> Buongiorno. Dove andate?

_____ Lei

> Sa l'indirizzo?

_____ Lei

> Mi dispiace ma posso accettare soltanto contanti.

_____ Lei

> Prego, la Sua ricevuta.

Activity C

What does the taxi driver say to you if…

1   …he wants to know the address of the hotel?

_____

2   …he is sorry?

_____

3   …you can only pay in cash?

_____

LESSON 6

Words to Know

Using a ticket machine

Here are the words you need to know to purchase tickets from an automatic ticket machine in the *metro*.

annullare	cancel
confermare	confirm
pagare	pay
Introdurre monete, banconote o carta di credito	Insert coins, bills or credit card
Selezionare il biglietto	Select ticket
biglietto singolo	single ticket
tariffa intera	full price
pacchetto da 10 biglietti	booklet of 10 tickets
Selezionare il numero di biglietti desiderato.	Select desired number of tickets.
Desidera la ricevuta?	Would you like a receipt?
Importo da pagare	Total due
Questa macchina dà il resto.	This machine returns change.
Resto massimo 4 €	Maximum change 4 €

CULTURE TIPS

- Before you take a bus or tram in Italy, buy your ticket at a ticket machine, a *tabacchi* (tobacconist's shop) or a newsstand. When you get on the bus don't give your ticket to the driver; instead there is a machine to validate your ticket (*obliterare/annullare/convalidare il biglietto*). Inspectors do come around and check if people have validated their tickets, so don't forget!

- You enter Italian buses through the front or back doors, marked *salire/entrata* (get on/entrance), and exit through the center door, marked *scendere/uscita* (get off/exit).

Activity A

For each image, would you select A or B if you wanted to…

1   …buy a subway ticket?

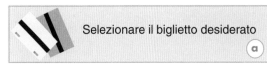

Selezionare il biglietto desiderato (a)

Ricarica la carta Metrebus (b)

2   …select "Cancel"?

Annulla (a)   (b)

3   …buy a booklet of tickets?

Biglietto singolo (a)

Pacchetto da 10 biglietti (b)

Activity B

Put the steps in the correct order to buy a ticket.

___ Selezionare "biglietto singolo"

___ Confermare

___ Introdurre monete, banconote o carta di credito

___ Ritirare (collect) biglietti

CULTURE TIP

Every municipality in Italy has a different system of public transport with its own prices and offers. In Rome you buy a *Metrebus-Ticket* which can be used for buses and subways. Tourist destinations usually have special tickets for tourists.

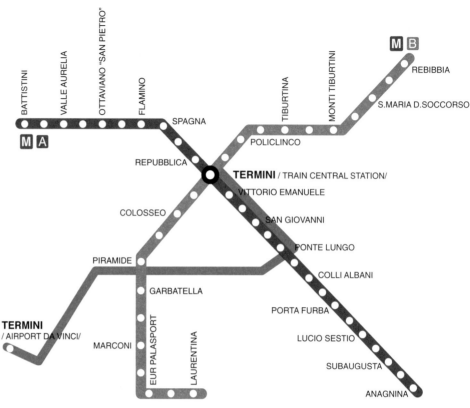

LESSON 7

Smart Phrases

Using the *metro*

Convalidi il biglietto.	Validate your ticket.
Prenda il ____.	Take bus number ____.
Prenda la linea B, direzione Laurentina.	Take line B toward Laurentina.
Salga a ____.	Get on at ____.
Scenda a ____.	Get off at ____.
Cambi a ____.	Change at ____.
Prosegua per ____ fermate.	Go ____ stops.
Arrivi al capolinea.	Go to the last stop.

SMART TIPS

- When someone tells you to get off at the first, second, third, etc. stop (*fermata*), he/she uses an ordinal number. The first ten ordinal numbers are: *primo, secondo, terzo, quarto, quinto, sesto, settimo, ottavo, nono, decimo.* Italian ordinal numbers agree in gender and number with the nouns they modify and are always preceded by the article: *il primo, la prima, i primi, le prime.*

- When Italians talk about buses, they say *Prenda il 12,* "Take the 12."

Activity A

Using the subway map, follow the directions to find the final destination.

1   Prenda la linea B alla stazione Garbatella, direzione Rebibbia.

2   Prosegua per cinque fermate e scenda a Termini.

3   Prenda la linea A, direzione Battistini.

4   Scenda al capolinea.

Dove sono?	Where am I?

_____

Activity B

Listen to the directions and find the final destination using the subway map.

1   Dove sono?

_____

2   Dove sono?

_____

LESSON 8

Smart Grammar

Definite/Indefinite Articles

You have already learned the definite articles *il, lo, la, l'* and *i, gli, le*. Now you will learn the indefinite articles *un, uno, una, un'*. While definite articles refer to something specific ("the plane," "the pilots"), indefinite articles are more general ("a plane"). Take a look at the following chart comparing definite and indefinite articles.

	Definite	**Indefinite**
m sing.	il, lo, l'	un, uno
f sing.	la, l'	una, un'
pl.	i, gli, le	

Example 1

Ho il biglietto.   I have the ticket.

Example 2

Ho un biglietto.   I have a ticket.

Example 1 refers to a specific ticket, while Example 2 refers to an unspecified ticket.

SMART TIPS

- Most masculine words take the indefinite article *un*; words that begin with *s* + consonant, *z–* or *gn–* take the indefinite article *uno*.

- The indefinite article *un* takes an apostrophe only in its feminine form. For example, you write *un aereo* (m), but *un'uscita* (f), even though both words begin with a vowel.

Activity A

Insert the correct definite article to refer to the pictures below.

1  _____ donna

2 _____ aereo

3 _____ bagaglio a mano

Activity B

Insert the correct indefinite article to refer to the pictures below.

1 _____ valigia

2 _____ uomo

3 _____ auto

Activity C

Fill in the blanks with the correct definite or indefinite article.

1   Ho soltanto _____ bagaglio a mano!

2   Prendo _____ metro.

3   Flavio ha _____ auto francese.

4   Questa macchina non dà _____ resto.

Activity A

Fill out the top of this Customs Declaration using your information.

DICHIARAZIONE DOGANALE

Cognome ....

Nome ....

Cittadinanza ....

Data di nascita ....

Luogo di nascita ....

Activity B

How would you ask…

1   …for a receipt in a taxi?

_____

2   …if you can pay by credit card?

_____

3   …what the address is?

_____

Challenge

Can you think of 5 different expressions that use the verb *avere*? Here's a hint: Don't be afraid!

_____

_____

_____

_____

_____

Activity C

Identify the items using the correct indefinite article.

1      _____

2   _____

3   _____

Activity D

Use the subway map from Lesson 7 to explain how to get…

1   …dalla stazione Tiburtina a Colli Albani.

_____

_____

2   …da piazza di Spagna a Laurentina.

_____

_____

_____

Internet Activity

Go online to **www.berlitzbooks.com/5Mtravel** where you will find a link to read about the different kinds of bus/subway tickets you can buy in Rome and the special offers for tourists. Check out the *bti* and *cis* tickets listed under *biglietti*.

Unit 4 Checking In

In this unit you will learn:
- how to check into a hotel room.
- negations and how to conjugate *–are* verbs.
- adjectives to describe your room.
- questions you might need to ask at the hotel.

LESSON 1

In albergo

Dialogue

Il sig. Mirabella has just arrived at the Hotel del Mare.
Listen to and follow along with the dialogue.

la receptionist	Buongiorno e benvenuto all'Hotel del Mare.
Sig. Mirabella	Buongiorno. Ho una prenotazione a nome di Marco Mirabella.
la receptionist	Sì, una camera doppia dal dodici al diciannove agosto.
Sig. Mirabella	Quanto costa a notte?
la receptionist	La doppia costa novanta euro a notte.

SMART TIP

The word *benvenuto* is used to welcome someone. For example, *Benvenuto in Italia* means "Welcome to Italy." It agrees with the number and gender of the people being addressed: *benvenuto/ benvenuta* (m/f sing.), *benvenuti/benvenute* (m/f pl.).

Activity A
Answer the following questions.

1   For how long is il sig. Mirabella staying at the Hotel del Mare? _____

2   How many people are staying in the room?

_____

3   How much does the room cost per night?

_____

Activity B
Read the dialogue again and look for cognates, or words that look similar in Italian and English.

1   _____

2   _____

3   _____

4   _____

Activity C
Answer the following questions.

1   Imagine that you are checking into a hotel. How would you present yourself?

_____

2   How would you ask how much the room is per night?

_____

LESSON 2

Words to Know

Core Words

l'aria condizionata	air conditioning
il bagno	bathroom
la camera	room
la connessione Internet wi-fi	wi-fi Internet access
la doccia	shower
il letto	bed
il piano	floor
il piano terra	ground floor
la scrivania	desk
il telefono	telephone
il televisore	television
la vasca	tub

Extra Words

il letto matrimoniale	double bed
il letto singolo	single bed
la sedia	chair

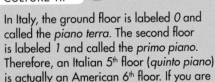

CULTURE TIP

In Italy, the ground floor is labeled 0 and called the *piano terra*. The second floor is labeled 1 and called the *primo piano*. Therefore, an Italian 5th floor (*quinto piano*) is actually an American 6th floor. If you are renting an apartment in Italy and it says "5th-floor walkup," just know that you'll be walking up six flights of stairs!

Activity A

Read the hotel confirmation and circle **T** for true or **F** for false.

Conferma di Prenotazione	
Hotel Villa Giulia ✦✦✦✦	• Camera al secondo piano • Bagno con vasca • Letto matrimoniale • Aria condizionata • Scrivania • Connessione Internet wi-fi

1	The hotel room is on the second floor.	T / F
2	There is a bathroom with a shower.	T / F
3	There is air conditioning.	T / F
4	There is wi-fi Internet access.	T / F
5	There is a single bed.	T / F

SMART TIP

Con means "with" and *senza* means "without." For example, *una camera con letto matrimoniale* means "a room with a double bed."

Activity B

Listen to the words and label the following images 1–4.

a

b

c

d

Activity A

What would you say if...

1 ...you needed an extra bed?

   _____

2 ...you made a reservation on the Internet?

   _____

3 ...you wanted to know if the hotel has a non-smoking room?

   _____

4 ...you wanted a room for two people, with a bathroom?

   _____

Core Phrases

Mi può consigliare un albergo?	Can you recommend a hotel?
Ho prenotato...	I made a reservation...
per telefono	on the phone
su Internet	on the Internet
con un'agenzia di viaggi	with a travel agency
Avete una camera...?	Do you have a room...?
singola/ doppia	for one person/ two people
con bagno	with a bathroom
con l'aria condizionata	with air conditioning
per fumatori/ non fumatori	that is smoking/ non-smoking
accessibile ai disabili	that is handicapped accessible
Quanto costa a notte?	How much is it a night?
Ho bisogno di...	I need...
un letto supplementare	an extra bed
un lettino	a crib
un letto matrimoniale	a double bed

Activity B

Match the questions to the answers that you hear from the hotel clerks. Label the questions 1–4.

_____ Avete una camera con l'aria condizionata?

_____ Quanto costa a notte?

_____ Avete una camera doppia?

_____ Avete una camera per non fumatori?

Your Turn

Imagine that you're planning your trip to Italy and you need to book a hotel room. Practice saying out loud what kind of room you need, and make sure to find out how much it costs!

SMART TIP

The Italian word for "hotel" is *albergo* even though "hotel" appears in almost all hotel names.

Negations

Negations are formed in Italian using the word *non*, which goes before the conjugated verb. For example:

C'è un letto.
There is a bed.

Non c'è il televisore.
There is no television.

Carlo è italiano.
Carlo is Italian.

Carlo non è francese.
Carlo is not French.

Quest'auto funziona.
This car works.

Quest'auto non funziona.
This car doesn't work.

Activity A

Rewrite each sentence in the negative.

1 La camera è al piano terra.

_____

2 Nella camera c'è il bagno.

_____

3 La doccia funziona.

_____

4 Ho bisogno di un lettino.

_____

> **SMART TIP**
>
> Italians often use double negation, formed with *non* and words with negative meaning, such as *nessuno* (no, none, nobody), *niente* (nothing) and *mai* (never). For example: *In camera non c'è nessuno* (There is nobody in the room); *Non abbiamo niente da fare* (We don't have anything to do); *Non vado mai in albergo* (I never go to a hotel).

Activity B

Answer each question in the negative.

1 Harry è italiano?

_____

2 Il telefono funziona?

_____

3 C'è la doccia?

_____

4 Peter parla italiano?

_____

LESSON 5

La mia camera

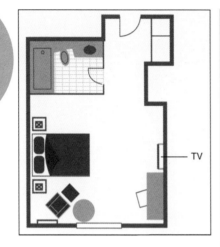

TV

My room

Lori has just checked into her hotel room. Here is a description of her *camera*.

Questa è la mia camera. È grande. Il letto è grande e comodo. Ci sono un televisore, una scrivania e una sedia. Nel bagno c'è la vasca.

Adjectives

grande	big
piccolo/piccola	small (m/f)
pulito/pulita	clean (m/f)
sporco/sporca	dirty (m/f)
comodo/comoda	comfortable (m/f)

SMART TIPS

- Adjectives, like articles, must agree with the nouns they describe. For example, *Il letto è comodo* (The bed is comfortable) and *La camera è comoda* (The room is comfortable). If the noun is plural, change the –o to –i for masculine, and the –a to –e for feminine. For example, *I letti sono comodi* (The beds are comfortable) and *Le camere sono comode* (The rooms are comfortable).

- If the adjective ends in –e, it doesn't change from masculine to feminine. For example, *Il letto è grande* (The bed is big) and *La camera è grande* (The room is big).

Activity A

Answer the questions about the hotel room.

1 Il letto è piccolo?

_____

2 C'è un televisore?

_____

3 Ci sono una sedia e una scrivania?

_____

SMART TIP

If you want to talk about your hotel room, you'll need to learn the possessive adjectives. Like adjectives, they agree with the noun that follows them (that is, with the thing that is possessed and not the possessor). In Italian, they are preceded by an article. This chart will help you:

	m sing.	f sing.	m pl.	f pl.
my	il mio	la mia	i miei	le mie
your	il tuo	la tua	i tuoi	le tue
your (form.)	il Suo	la Sua	i Suoi	le Sue
his/her/its	il suo	la sua	i suoi	le sue
our	il nostro	la nostra	i nostri	le nostre
your (pl.)	il vostro	la vostra	i vostri	le vostre
their	il loro	la loro	i loro	le loro

Activity B

Fill in the blanks with the correct possessive adjective.

1 _____ bagno è molto piccolo. (my)

2 _____ doccia non funziona. (their)

3 _____ letto è comodo. (his/her)

4 _____ camere non sono grandi. (your pl.)

LESSON 6
Words to Know

Core Words

l'ascensore	elevator [lift] (m)
l'asciugamano	towel
la carta igienica	toilet paper
la chiave	key
la coperta	blanket
il cuscino	pillow
il lavandino	sink
il lenzuolo/le lenzuola	sheet/sheets
la saponetta	soap
la scala	staircase
lo shampoo	shampoo

Extra Words

il bollitore	electric kettle
il ferro da stiro	iron
il fon	hairdryer

Activity A

Listen to the words and circle each picture that the speaker says. At the end, there should be one picture that isn't circled.

Write the Italian word of the one picture left. _____

Activity B
Che disastro!

What a disaster! Thomas and Kathleen have just checked into their room and so many things are missing. Use the pictures below to say what is missing.

1   Non ci sono gli _____.

2   Non c'è la _____.

3   Non c'è lo _____.

4   Non c'è la _____.

> **SMART TIP**
>
> If you need more of something, say *Ho bisogno di un altro/un'altra* ____. If you need one more towel, say *Ho bisogno di un altro asciugamano*. If you need more than one of something, use the plural forms *altri/altre*. To ask for more blankets, for example, say *Ho bisogno di due altre coperte*, "I need two more blankets."

Activity C

Complete the word webs with objects that belong in either *la camera* or *il bagno*.

la camera   *il bagno*

Core Phrases

Non disturbare.	Do not disturb.
Potrei avere due asciugamani puliti?	Can I have two clean towels?
Mi può svegliare alle _____?	Can I get a wake-up call at _____?
Mi può consigliare un buon ristorante?	Could you recommend a good restaurant?
Mi può chiamare un taxi?	Could you call me a taxi?
A che ora devo lasciare la camera?	What time is check-out?
C'è il servizio lavanderia?	Do you have laundry service?
Mi può rifare la camera?	Can you have my room cleaned?
Ho lasciato la chiave in camera.	I left my key in the room.

SMART PRONUNCIATION

You might have noticed that some Italian words have an accent. In most cases the accent mark shows which vowel is stressed, as with the word *può* (pronounced *pwoh*). In the case of the verb *è* (you are/he/she is), the accent distinguishes it from the word *e* (and).

Activity A

What do you say if you want…

1   …a wake-up call at 7:00AM?

   _____

2   …the hotel to call you a taxi?

   _____

3   …to know what time check-out is?

   _____

4   …to have your room cleaned?

   _____

Activity B

Listen to the questions and label the photos 1–4 after deciding who is speaking.

   _____   _____

   _____   _____

LESSON 8

Smart Grammar

Regular –are verbs

Regular verbs in Italian end in either –are, –ere or –ire. There are also many irregular verbs that you will learn and have already learned, such as andare, essere and avere. In this lesson you will learn how to conjugate regular –are verbs.

To begin, remove the –are ending, and then add the following endings:

	visitare	**to visit**
(io)	visit**o**	I visit
(tu)	visit**i**	you visit
(Lei)	visit**a**	you visit
(lui/lei)	visit**a**	he/she visits
(noi)	visit**iamo**	we visit
(voi)	visit**ate**	you visit
(loro)	visit**ano**	they visit

Here are some regular –are verbs:

amare	to love
arrivare	to arrive
ascoltare	to listen to
ballare	to dance
camminare	to walk
cercare	to look for
domandare	to ask (for)
guardare	to look at
lavorare	to work
parlare	to speak/to talk
restare	to stay
studiare	to study
trovare	to find

Activity A

Conjugate the verb parlare, to speak.

io _____

tu _____

Lei _____

lui/lei _____

noi _____

voi _____

loro _____

Activity B

Fill in the blanks with the correct conjugated verb.

1 Marco e Anna _____ inglese.
parlare

2 _____ la Torre di Pisa.
noi, visitare

3 _____ italiano.
io, studiare

4 Caterina _____ in albergo.
restare

5 _____ un buon ristorante.
Lei, cercare

Activity C

Match the pronoun on the left with its verb on the right.

1	io	a	parliamo
2	tu	b	visitano
3	noi	c	resto
4	voi	d	studi
5	loro	e	cercate

SMART PRONUNCIATION

The forms cerchi (you look for) and cerchiamo (we look for) have an h before the letter c to show you that it is pronounced /k/.

Activity A

Label the following images.

1

_____

2

_____

3

_____

4

_____

Activity B

Rewrite each sentence in the negative.

1 Lei studia spagnolo.

_____

2 Il ferro da stiro funziona.

_____

3 Visitiamo il Vaticano.

_____

4 Le nostre camere sono piccole.

_____

Activity C

Translate the phrases into Italian.

1 my telephone _____

2 his room _____

3 their blankets _____

4 your (sing.) key _____

Activity D

Find the following words related to hotels in the word search.

ascensore	letto	piccola
scrivania	doccia	piano
camera	saponetta	singolo
chiave	televisore	sedia
comoda	vasca	doppia

```
D R T P P C S A M G S L S B G
C O M O D A W Q X A I M K L P
F Z Q M K L S A P O N E T T A
S D J L P F C B E S G D S E S
K Y P G T V R K D C O C C L X
P N I E E S I R C Z L Z R E Z
O M C H I A V E A A O S U V X
W O C Q C V A D V C D T T I V
V L O A V I N F K A K E E S G
Z I L Z O T I W Y M P I D O L
P I A N O E A S C E N S O R E
M U P T M Z P C G R U E V E T
Y N R U S V C U V A H D X D T
P V A S C A R I C D V I A B O
Q G T O Z X D O P P I A Q N T
```

Challenge

Now that you know how to conjugate –are verbs, can you conjugate the following verbs: *domandare*, *ballare*, *lavorare* and *amare*?

Internet Activity

Go online to **www.berlitzbooks.com/5Mtravel** to find a list of some of Italy's hotel chains. Browse through their websites and see if you can understand what kinds of rooms and services they offer.

Unit 5 Around Town

In this unit you will learn how to:
- talk about different places to visit.
- conjugate the verbs *vedere* (to see) and *potere* (to be able to, can).
- get and follow directions.
- ask many different kinds of questions.

In città

Dialogue

Listen to the following dialogue of a couple deciding on what to do during their stay in Rome.

Anna	Che facciamo oggi?
Francesco	Prima dobbiamo andare in banca.
Anna	Dopo possiamo andare a visitare il Colosseo?
Francesco	Sì! Io vorrei visitare anche una chiesa.
Anna	A Roma c'è sempre molto da fare!

SMART TIPS

- The Italian question for "What are we going to do today?" is *Che cosa facciamo oggi?* However, when Italians speak they often leave out *cosa* and just say *che*. For example, *Che fai domani?*, "What are you going to do tomorrow?" instead of *Che cosa fai domani?*.

- To say "First we have to do something," Italians say *prima.* "Afterwards" is *dopo*.

Activity A
Circle **T** for true and **F** for false.

1 Francesco e Anna sono in vacanza.   **T / F**

2 Vanno a visitare un museo.   **T / F**

3 Vanno a visitare il Colosseo.   **T / F**

4 A Roma non c'è niente da fare.   **T / F**

Activity B
Listen to the dialogue again and fill in the missing words.

_____ facciamo oggi?

Prima dobbiamo andare _____.

Dopo possiamo andare a _____ il Colosseo?

Sì! Io vorrei visitare anche _____.

A Roma _____ sempre molto da fare!

LESSON 2

Words to Know

Core Words

la banca	bank
il castello	castle
la chiesa	church
il Comune	town hall [council]
la fontana	fountain
il mercato	market
il monumento	monument
il museo	museum
il parco	park
la piazza	town square
il ponte	bridge
l'ufficio del turismo	tourism office
l'Ufficio Postale	post office

Activity A

Label the following buildings.

1 _____

2 _____

3 _____

4 _____

Activity B

Where can you find the following?

1 maps of the city, information on tours, brochures

   _____

2 fresh flowers, food, wine and cheese

   _____

3 grass, trees, paths for walking

   _____

4 paintings, sculptures, gift shops

   _____

Activity C

Match the Italian words with their English equivalents.

1	il museo	a	post office
2	il ponte	b	town square
3	l'Ufficio Postale	c	bridge
4	la piazza	d	museum
5	il parco	e	market
6	il mercato	f	park

Your Turn

Use your new vocabulary to make a list of places you want to visit.

DA VEDERE
TO SEE

1. _____
2. _____
3. _____
4. _____

Smart Phrases

Core Phrases

Dov'è …?	Where is …?
il bancomat più vicino	the nearest ATM
una banca	the bank
un ufficio di cambio	the currency exchange office
Vorrei cambiare	I want to exchange
… in euro.	…for euros.
dei dollari	dollars
delle sterline	pounds
dei travel cheque	traveler's checks
Qual è il tasso di cambio?	What is the exchange rate?
Il bancomat mi ha preso la carta.	The ATM ate my card.
A che ora apre/chiude la banca?	What time does the bank open/close?

Activity A

Fill in the blanks with the correct currency in Italian.

1 Vorrei cambiare dei _____ in
                       $
  _____.
    €

2 Vorrei cambiare delle _____ in
                         £
  _____.
    $

3 Vorrei cambiare degli _____ in
                         €
  _____.
    £

Activity B

Listen to the questions and write the number next to the correct answer.

___ La banca apre alle 9.

___ Il tasso di cambio è di 1 euro per 1 dollaro e quaranta.

___ C'è un bancomat vicino alla banca.

___ La banca chiude alle 16.30.

Activity C

What do you say if…

1 …the ATM ate your card.

_____

2 …you want to know when the bank opens?

_____

3 …you want to exchange travelers checks for euros?

_____

4 …you want to know where the nearest ATM is?

_____

5 …you want to know the exchange rate?

_____

6 …you want to know what time the bank closes?

_____

Your Turn

Now that you can talk about exchanging money in Italian, practice saying that you need to exchange money from your country's currency for euros.

LESSON 4

Smart Grammar

The verbs *vedere* and *potere*

The verb *vedere* is regular in the present tense.

	vedere	**to see**
(io)	vedo	I see
(tu)	vedi	you see
(Lei)	vede	you see
(lui/lei)	vede	he/she sees
(noi)	vediamo	we see
(voi)	vedete	you see
(loro)	vedono	they see

The verb *potere* is irregular. The chart shows its conjugation in the present tense.

	potere	**to be able to, can**
(io)	posso	I can
(tu)	puoi	you can
(Lei)	può	you can
(lui/lei)	può	he/she can
(noi)	possiamo	we can
(voi)	potete	you can
(loro)	possono	they can

SMART TIP

The verb *potere* can be followed by an infinitive if you want to say "to be able to do something." For example, *Possiamo visitare il museo* means "We are able to (we can) visit the museum."

Activity A

Write a sentence in Italian telling what the following people see.

1   (io, il castello) _____

2   (Giuseppe, il mercato) _____

3   (noi, il ponte) _____

4   (voi, la piazza) _____

Activity B

Conjugate the verb *potere*, to be able to.

io   _____

tu   _____

Lei   _____

lui/lei   _____

noi   _____

voi   _____

loro   _____

Activity C

Fill in the blanks with the correct verb form.

1   _____ (noi, potere) andare prima al Colosseo.

2   _____ (Lei, vedere) la fermata dell'autobus?

3   _____ (Lei, potere) prendere il 14 e scendere in via di Ripetta.

4   Non _____ (io, vedere) nessun bancomat.

Activity D

Answer the following questions in the affirmative.

1   Può andare in vacanza?

   _____

2   Può visitare il museo?

   _____

3   Possiamo visitare il Comune?

   _____

4   Vedi un bancomat?

   _____

5   L'ufficio di cambio può cambiare dei dollari in euro?

   _____

6   Posso andare in banca?

   _____

Indicazioni

Dialogue

Listen to the following dialogue to learn how to ask for and understand directions.

Uomo Mi scusi, per andare a piazza Navona?

Donna Prenda la seconda a destra poi vada sempre dritto. Piazza Navona è sulla sinistra. La vede subito.

Uomo Grazie mille!

Donna Prego.

SMART TIPS

- Here are some words you may need to get directions:

a sinistra	on/to the left	*continui*	continue
a destra	on/to the right	*attraversi*	cross
sempre dritto	straight ahead	*sulla*	on
prenda	take	*verso*	toward
giri	turn		

- When giving directions to strangers, Italians use the polite command verb forms given above, which are slightly different from the present tense. You don't need to learn them, but you might hear them.

Activity A

How would someone tell you to…

1 …turn left?

_____

2 …continue straight ahead?

_____

3 …turn right?

_____

4 …take your second left?

_____

SMART TIPS

- *Prego* is the most common way of saying "you're welcome" in Italian. Another way to say "you're welcome" is *di niente* (literally, "it's nothing").

- *Prego* is also used to invite somebody to do something. *Posso?* or *Permesso?* means "May I come through?" and a polite answer is *Prego* (by all means!).

- You can also use *prego* as a polite way to ask someone to repeat himself.

- In a shop or restaurant you may be asked *Prego?* meaning "Can I help you?"

Activity B

Look at the map below and follow the directions. Where is the final destination?

1 Siete vicino a Piazza Colonna. Prendete via del Corso, a destra. Girate alla prima a sinistra: è via dei Sabini. Girate a destra su via di Santa Maria in Via. Poi prendete via delle Muratte, la prima a sinistra. Andate sempre dritto e arrivate alla Fontana.

Siamo a _____.

2 Partite da via del Tritone. Andate sempre dritto e arrivate a largo Chigi. Girate a sinistra su via del Corso. Girate alla prima destra: il palazzo è lì.

Siamo a _____.

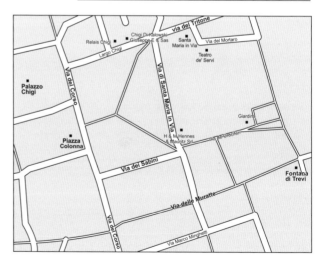

Words to Know

L'euro (The euro)

la banconota	bill
il centesimo	cent
in contanti	in cash
la moneta	coin
i soldi	money (pl.)
gli spicci	change (pl.)

I numeri (Numbers)

You already know how to count from 1–60. Now you will learn from 70 on.

settanta	70
settantuno	71
settantadue	72
settantatré	73
settantaquattro	74
settantacinque	75
settantasei	76
settantasette	77
settantotto	78
settantanove	79
ottanta	80
ottantuno	81
ottantadue	82
novanta	90
novantuno	91
novantadue	92
cento	100
mille	1,000
duemila	2,000

SMART TIP

As you have noticed in *duemila* (2,000), the plural form of *mille* (1,000) is *mila*. 3,000, 4,000 etc. are *tremila*, *quattromila* etc.

Activity A

Write how much money there is in each picture.

1 _____

2 _____

3 _____

4 _____

SMART TIPS

- The period and commas are inverted in Italian prices. For example, $1,000.00 in English would be *$1.000,00* in Italian.
- To ask how much something costs, say *Quanto costa?*
- When you go to the cashier and want to know how much you have to pay, ask *Quant'è?* (How much is it?).

Activity B

Write out the following prices in words.

1 €1.500,60 _____

2 €99,99 _____

3 €0,75 _____

Smart Phrases

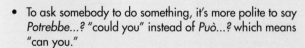

Core Phrases

Mi sono perso/persa.	I am lost. (m/f)
Mi scusi, cerco…	Excuse me, I am looking for…
Per favore, potrebbe…?	Could you please…?
parlare più lentamente	speak more slowly
ripetere	repeat that
dirmi come si scrive	spell it for me
scriverlo	write it down
indicarlo sulla cartina	show me on the map
indicarmi la strada	give me directions
Mi dispiace ma non ho capito.	I'm sorry, I didn't understand.
Che significa?	What does that mean?

Activity A

Match the audio with what each person is saying.

a. I'm lost.

b. Can you speak more slowly? #__

#__

d. Can you spell it? #__

c. I'm looking for piazza Navona.

#__

Activity B

What do you say if…

1 …you want someone to repeat what they said?
_____

2 …you don't understand the word *il ponte*?
_____

3 …you (female) are lost?
_____

4 …you don't understand?
_____

5 …you want someone to show you on the map?
_____

6 …you are looking for the bank?
_____

7 …you want someone to speak more slowly?
_____

8 …you want someone to give you directions?
_____

Your Turn

Imagine that you're having a difficult time understanding someone in Italian. What can you say to the person so that he or she can help you understand better?

LESSON 8

Smart Grammar

Question Words

The following words will help you ask questions in Italian.

che cosa	what
chi	who
come	how
dove	where
perché	why
quando	when
quanto	how much
quanti/quante	how many (m/f pl.)

SMART TIPS

- Another way of asking someone to repeat himself in Italian is *Come?* If you don't understand something, you can say *Come, scusi?* It is polite and less formal than *Prego?*

- *Dove, quanto* and *cosa* form contractions with the verb *è*, "is." For example: *Dov'è...?* "Where is ...?" *Quant'è?* "How much is it?" *Che cos'è?* "What is it?"

Activity A

Write the question word associated with each image.

1

_____

2

_____

3

_____

4

_____

Activity B

Complete the questions with the correct question word.

1 _____ costa?

2 _____ si chiama?

3 _____ è una banca?

4 _____ c'è in auto con Francesca?

Activity C

Match the English question words with their Italian equivalents.

1	what		a	come
2	how much		b	dove
3	when		c	perché
4	where		d	quanto
5	why		e	che (cosa)
6	how		f	quando

Activity D

Complete the crossword puzzle with the Italian equivalents of the words provided.

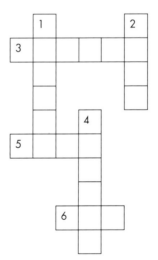

Across

3 when

5 where

6 who

Down

1 how much

2 how

4 why

Unit 5 Review

Activity A
Label these different *monumenti* and *cose da vedere*.

1
_____

2
_____

3
_____

4
_____

Activity B
Fill in the blanks with the correct form of the verb *potere*.

1 (noi) _____ visitare la chiesa.

2 (voi) _____ andare in vacanza.

3 (io) _____ pagare?

4 (loro) _____ vedere il ponte.

Activity C
Complete the conjugation table for the verb *vedere*.

io	
	vedi
Lei	
lui/lei	
	vediamo
voi	
loro	

Activity D
What do you say if...

1 ...you want someone to speak more slowly?

_____

2 ...you want someone to write something down?

_____

3 ...you want to know how much something costs?

_____

4 ...you want to know where the church is?

_____

Activity E
Match the Italian words with their English equivalents.

1 dove   a to see
2 vedere   b when
3 il mercato   c to the right
4 quando   d where
5 la banca   e to be able to
6 potere   f bank
7 a destra   g market

Challenge
Can you read the following numbers out loud without stopping?

1 692
2 1399
3 2010
4 77

Internet Activity
Go online to **www.berlitzbooks.com/5Mtravel** where you will find a link to online maps of Italy. Put in the address of a hotel in Rome and then the address of a museum. See if you can understand the directions. If you want to get walking directions, make sure you choose *a piedi*, "by foot."

In this unit you will learn:
- **how to find a good restaurant.**
- **different food and drink.**
- **how to order in a café or restaurant.**
- **the verbs** *prendere* **(to take),** *volere* **(to want) and** *bere* **(to drink).**

LESSON 1

Andiamo a mangiare!

Dialogue

Listen to the following dialogue between Edward and the concierge.

Edward	Mi può consigliare un ristorante?
Portiere	Le piace la pizza?
Edward	Sì, mi piace tutta la cucina italiana.
Portiere	C'è una buona pizzeria accanto all'Ufficio Postale.
Edward	È lontano?
Portiere	No, l'Ufficio Postale è di fronte alla chiesa.

CULTURE TIP

A *pizzeria* is a typical Italian restaurant that serves a variety of *pizzas* and other local food. The setting is relaxed and the prices are reasonable.

SMART TIP

Here are some more words to help with directions:

accanto a	next to
davanti a	in front of
dietro a	behind
di fronte a	across from
lontano da	far from
vicino a	close to

Activity A
Complete the following sentences based on the dialogue.

1 Edward cerca _____.

2 A Edward piace tutta _____.

3 L'Ufficio Postale è _____ chiesa.

Activity B
Answer the questions in Italian.

1 A Edward piace la cucina spagnola?

   _____

2 C'è una pizzeria accanto all'Uffico Postale?

   _____

3 La pizzeria è lontano dall'Uffico Postale?

   _____

Activity C
Match the prepositions with their English equivalents.

1	lontano da	a	close to
2	accanto a	b	far from
3	di fronte a	c	in front of
4	vicino a	d	next to
5	davanti a	e	across from

SMART TIP

In English, you say that A likes B. In Italian, B is pleasing to A. The verb *piacere* (to like) is mostly used in the 3rd person: *piace* when referring to a singular noun, *piacciono* when the noun is plural. The person who likes something is expressed by a pronoun: *mi piace la pizza*, for example, means "I like pizza", *Le piacciono gli spaghetti?* is "Do you like spaghetti?"

Words to Know

Core Words

la colazione	breakfast
il pranzo	lunch
la cena	dinner

Antipasti — **Appetizers**

l'antipasto misto — assorted appetizer plate
l'insalata di frutti di mare — seafood salad
prosciutto e melone — cured ham and melon

Primi piatti — **First courses**

le fettuccine — egg pasta
gli gnocchi — small potato dumplings
le lasagne — lasagna
gli spaghetti — spaghetti
i tortellini — tortellini
la minestra — soup

Pesce — **Fish**

le cozze — mussels
i gamberetti — shrimp
il merluzzo — cod
il salmone — salmon
la sogliola — sole

Carne — **Meat**

l'agnello — lamb
la bistecca — steak
il maiale — pork
il manzo — beef
il pollo — chicken

Contorni — **Vegetables**

i carciofi — artichokes
l'insalata — salad
le melanzane — eggplants
i peperoni — peppers
le patate — potatoes

Dessert — **Desserts**

il dolce — cake
il gelato — ice cream
il formaggio — cheese
la frutta — fruit
la torta — pie

Activity A

Label the food on the table below.

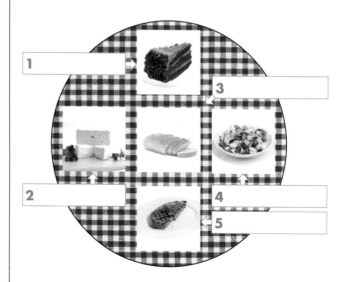

1

3

2

4

5

Activity B

Fill in the table with food you like and don't like.

mi piace/piacciono	non mi piace/piacciono

CULTURE TIPS

- On the menu of an Italian restaurant you can usually find *pane e coperto* (bread and cover charge) which is a fixed price. *Il servizio* (service charge) is sometimes included in *pane e coperto*, but don't be surprised if you sometimes find it as a separate charge on your bill.

- Did you notice that cheese is under the *desserts* category? The order of food in a typical Italian meal is: *antipasto, primo, secondo, contorno, dessert*.

LESSON 3
Smart Phrases

Core Phrases

Io prendo _____.	I'll have the _____.
Mi può portare…?	Could you bring me…?
il conto	the check
un coltello	a knife
un cucchiaio	a spoon
una forchetta	a fork
un tovagliolo	a napkin
un bicchiere	a glass
Ci può portare una bottiglia d'acqua?	Could you bring us a bottle of water?
Avete il menù in inglese?	Do you have an English menu?
Sono…	I am…
allergico/allergica a…	allergic to… (m/f)
vegetariano/vegetariana	vegetarian (m/f)
vegano/vegana	vegan (m/f)
Dov'è la toilette?	Where are the bathrooms?

Activity A
Label the following items in Italian.

1 _____

2 _____

3 _____

4 _____

Activity B
What's missing from this table setting? Ask the waiter for what you need!

1 _____

2 _____

3 _____

Activity C
How do you…

1 …say you're a vegetarian?

_____

2 …ask for the check?

_____

3 …ask where the bathrooms are?

_____

4 …order the salad?

_____

Your Turn
Now that you know how to order in a restaurant, use the vocabulary you've learned to practice ordering your favorite meal out loud. Don't forget to order something to drink, too!

Smart Grammar

The verb *prendere*, to take

The verb *prendere* is regular. The chart shows its conjugation in the present tense.

	prendere	to take
(io)	prendo	I take
(tu)	prendi	you take
(Lei)	prende	you take
(lui/lei)	prende	he/she takes
(noi)	prendiamo	we take
(voi)	prendete	you take
(loro)	prendono	they take

Activity A

Fill in the blanks with the correct form of *prendere*.

1   Loro che cosa _____ ?

2   (Tu) _____ gli spaghetti o le lasagne?

3   (io) _____ il pollo con l'insalata.

4   (noi) _____ il dessert?

5   (voi) _____ un taxi per andare al ristorante?

SMART TIPS

- When you order food in Italian, use the verb *prendere* (to take) and not the verb *avere* (to have).

- If you want to use the word "or" in Italian, say *o*. For example, *Prende la carne o il pesce?* "Are you having meat or fish?" Note that *o* (or) is different than *ho* (I have), though they're pronounced almost the same.

Activity B

Say what each person is ordering. Don't forget to use the correct form of *prendere*!

1

Carlo _____ .

2

Noi _____ .

3

Voi _____ .

4

Loro _____ .

Activity C

Answer the following questions in Italian.

1   Un vegetariano prende la carne o l'insalata?

_____

2   Per andare in Italia (Lei) prende l'autobus o l'aereo?

_____

3   Con la carne gli italiani prendono un contorno o un dessert?

_____

4   Prendiamo un gelato come dessert o come antipasto?

_____

Al ristorante

Dialogue

Cristina and Martino are trying to decide what to eat *al ristorante* (at the restaurant). Listen to their conversation.

Cristina	Che cosa prendi?
Martino	Io prendo le lasagne e i carciofi. E tu?
Cristina	Io prendo il menù del giorno.
Martino	Com'è?
Cristina	Antipasto misto, spaghetti al pomodoro, bistecca e insalata.
Martino	E il dessert non c'è?
Cristina	Sì: gelato di frutta.
Martino	Prendiamo anche una bottiglia di vino?
Cristina	Volentieri!

CULTURE TIP

Many restaurants in Italy have a *menù del giorno* (prix-fixe menu) where the first and second courses, vegetable, water and dessert are included in the price. Depending on the restaurant it can include an appetizer, too.

SMART TIP

How do you like your steak? If you like it rare, say *al sangue*; if you like it medium, say *media*; if you like it well-done, say *ben cotta*.

Activity A

Match Cristina and Martino with the food they're going to order.

Activity B

What would you say if you want to order…

1 …a prix-fixe menu?

　＿＿＿＿＿＿＿＿＿＿＿＿＿＿＿＿＿＿＿＿＿＿

2 …ice cream for dessert?

　＿＿＿＿＿＿＿＿＿＿＿＿＿＿＿＿＿＿＿＿＿＿

3 …the steak (well-done)?

　＿＿＿＿＿＿＿＿＿＿＿＿＿＿＿＿＿＿＿＿＿＿

4 …a bottle of wine?

　＿＿＿＿＿＿＿＿＿＿＿＿＿＿＿＿＿＿＿＿＿＿

LESSON 6

Words to Know

 Core Words

Le bevande (Drinks)

l'acqua	water
la birra	beer
il caffè	coffee
il caffè macchiato	coffee "marked" with a little milk
il cappuccino	cappuccino
la cioccolata calda	hot chocolate
la coca-cola/ coca-cola light	cola/diet cola
il latte	milk
il succo d'arancia	orange juice
il tè	tea
il tè freddo	iced tea
il vino bianco/rosso	white/red wine

CULTURE TIP

If you order a *caffè* in Italy, you'll get an espresso. If you want a less-concentrated coffee ask for a *caffè lungo*, and if you want an American-style coffee, say *un caffè americano*.

Activity A

Che cosa prendono? Complete the sentences with the correct form of *prendere* and the name of the drink.

1 Emma _____.

2 Carla e Michela _____.

3 Noi _____.

Activity B

Complete the crossword puzzle with the Italian equivalents of the words provided.

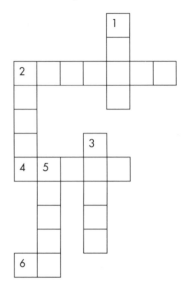

Across	Down
2 drinks	1 wine
4 water	2 beer
6 tea	3 less concentrated coffee
	5 coffee

Activity C

Write what you like to drink with each meal.

la colazione

_____

il pranzo

_____

la cena

_____

Activity D

Match the Italian words with their English equivalents.

1	il tè	a	milk
2	la birra	b	tea
3	il latte	c	coffee
4	l'acqua	d	cola
5	la coca-cola	e	water
6	il caffè	f	beer

Core Phrases

Prego?	How can I help you?
Che cosa desidera?	What would you like?
Desidera…?	Would you like…?
un aperitivo	a cocktail/before-dinner drink
un digestivo	a liqueur/after-dinner drink
un'acqua gassata	sparkling water
un'acqua naturale	still water
A Lei!	Here it is!
Buon appetito!	Enjoy your meal!
Desidera altro?	Would you like anything else?

SMART TIP

When addressing people at a table, an Italian waiter may use *Loro*, which is more formal than the usual *voi*. In this case the questions would be *Che cosa desiderano?* and *Desiderano…?*

CULTURE TIP

In Italy, it is customary to leave some extra change (no more than 1 or 2 euros) for the *mancia*, or "tip," if you are happy with the service. In a good restaurant you can leave more.

Activity A

Put these questions/phrases you might hear from a waiter in the correct order.

_____ Buon appetito!

_____ Desidera altro?

_____ Che cosa desidera?

_____ A Lei!

Activity B

Fill in the blanks with the correct Italian word.

1 Desidera _____ (still water)?

2 Desidera _____ (a cocktail)?

3 Desidera _____ (sparkling water)?

4 Desidera _____ (a liqueur)?

Activity C

Make up answers to the following questions and say them out loud.

Che cosa desidera?

Lei _____

Desidera altro?

Lei _____

Smart Grammar

The verbs *volere* (to want) and *bere* (to drink)

The verbs *volere* and *bere* are irregular. The charts below show their conjugations:

	volere	**to want**
(io)	voglio	I want
(tu)	vuoi	you want
(Lei)	vuole	you want
(lui/lei)	vuole	he/she wants
(noi)	vogliamo	we want
(voi)	volete	you want
(loro)	vogliono	they want

	bere	**to drink**
(io)	bevo	I drink
(tu)	bevi	you drink
(Lei)	beve	you drink
(lui/lei)	beve	he/she drinks
(noi)	beviamo	we drink
(voi)	bevete	you drink
(loro)	bevono	they drink

SMART TIPS

- The conjugated verb *volere* is often followed by an infinitive to mean ".to want to do something." For example, *Che cosa vuoi mangiare?* "What do you want to eat?"

- If you want your salad with *olio* (oil) but without *aceto* (vinegar), or some dessert after your coffee, you'll need to learn some new prepositions. Here are some useful prepositions:

prima	before
dopo	after
con	with
senza	without

Activity A

Complete the conjugation table for the verb *volere*.

io	
tu	
Lei	
lui/lei	
noi	
voi	
loro	

Activity B

Complete the conjugation table for the verb *bere*.

io	
tu	
Lei	
lui/lei	
noi	
voi	
loro	

Activity C

Fill in the blanks with the correct form of *volere*.

1 Massimo _____ andare in vacanza.

2 (io) _____ un'acqua gassata.

3 Cinzia e Luigi _____ un cappuccino.

4 (noi) _____ andare al ristorante.

Activity D

Fill in the blanks with the correct form of *bere*.

1 A cena Marta _____ vino rosso.

2 (tu) _____ acqua naturale.

3 (Lei) _____ il caffè dopo cena?

4 (loro) _____ un aperitivo prima di pranzo.

Unit 6 Review

Activity A
How do you...

1 ...ask for the check?

_____

2 ...order the chicken?

_____

3 ...say that you drink coffee?

_____

4 ...ask where the bathroom is?

_____

Activity B
Label the following food and drink.

1

_____

2

_____

3

_____

4

_____

Activity C
Choose the word that doesn't belong in each group.

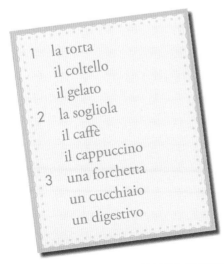

1 la torta
   il coltello
   il gelato
2 la sogliola
   il caffè
   il cappuccino
3 una forchetta
   un cucchiaio
   un digestivo

Activity D
Write the Italian translation of each word, and then arrange the circled letters to find a bonus word.

1 cheese: ___ ___ ___ (○) ___ ___ ___ ___
2 bread: (○) ___ ___ ___ ___
3 pie: ___ ___ (○) ___ ___ ___
4 ice cream: ___ ___ ___ (○) ___ ___
5 sole: (○) ___ ___ ___ ___ ___ ___

Bonus word: ___ ___ ___ ___ ___

Activity E
Fill in the blanks with the correct form of the verb given.

1 Massimo _____ (volere) bere un'acqua naturale.

2 _____ (noi, bere) succo d'arancia.

3 _____ (Lei, prendere) il pesce?

4 _____ (loro, volere) andare al ristorante.

5 Dopo pranzo _____ (io, bere) un caffè.

6 _____ (tu, prendere) un gelato?

> **Challenge**
> Can you conjugate the verbs *prendere, volere* and *bere* without checking in the book?

Internet Activity

Go online to **www.berlitzbooks.com/5Mtravel** where you will find the links to some restaurants in Italy. Check out the menus and start planning your dinner ahead of time!

Unit 7 Shopping & Souvenirs

In this unit you will learn:
- how to shop in Italy.
- ideas for souvenirs.
- new adjectives and how to use them.
- how to conjugate *–ere* and *–ire* verbs.

LESSON 1

Facciamo shopping!

The Souvenir Shop

Emma is in a souvenir shop looking for presents for her friends.

SMART TIP

The word *souvenir* is actually a French word, which means "a memory."

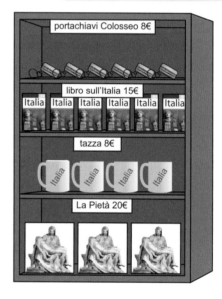

Activity A
What can Emma buy for…?

1 Rick – *gli piace l'arte*

_____

2 Sarah – *le piace la moda* (fashion)

_____

3 Thomas – *gli piace leggere* (to read)

_____

4 Monica – *le piace prendere il tè*

_____

Activity B
Emma only has 20€. Is that enough to buy…

1 la palla di neve e il cappellino? **Sì/No**

2 La Pietà e la tazza? **Sì/No**

3 la T-shirt e il libro? **Sì/No**

4 la miniatura e il portachiavi? **Sì/No**

Activity C
Which souvenirs would you buy for your friends?

1 _____
2 _____
3 _____
4 _____

LESSON 2
Words to Know

Core Words

l'alimentari	grocery store
la boutique	boutique
il centro commerciale	shopping mall [centre]
l'enoteca	wine store
la farmacia	pharmacy
il fioraio	flower shop
la gioielleria	jewelry store [jeweller's]
il grande magazzino	department store
la libreria	bookstore
il negozio…	…store [shop]
di abbigliamento	clothing
di antiquariato	antique
di scarpe	shoe
di souvenir	souvenir
la panetteria	bakery
la pasticceria	pastry shop
la pelletteria	leather goods store
la profumeria	perfume store
il supermercato	supermarket
la tabaccheria	tobacco shop [smoke shop]

CULTURE TIPS

- Some of the most popular department stores in Italy include *Coin*, *Rinascente* and *Oviesse* and some of the most popular supermarkets are *GS*, *SMA* and *Pam*.

- There is much more than just cigarettes in a *tabaccheria*. You can find phone cards, stamps and bus and *metro* tickets.

Activity A
Label each of the stores below.

1

_____

2

_____

3

_____

4
_____

Activity B
Fill in the blanks with the correct store names.

1 Cecilia e Alessandra cercano _____.
the shopping mall

2 Cerco _____.
the shoe store

3 Cerca _____.
the bookstore

4 Cerchiamo _____.
the perfume store

Activity C
Match each item with the store where you can buy it.

1	earrings	a	l'enoteca
2	flowers	b	la gioielleria
3	perfume	c	la farmacia
4	wine	d	il fioraio
5	aspirin	e	la profumeria

LESSON 3
Smart Phrases

Core Phrases

Posso vedere questo/quello?	Can I see this/that?
Volevo solo dare un'occhiata.	I'm just browsing.
Quanto costa?	How much does it cost?
Posso pagare con la carta di credito?	Can I pay with a credit card?
Dov'è la cassa?	Where is the cashier?
È troppo caro.	It's too expensive.
Ho soltanto ____ euro.	I only have ____ euros.
Mi può fare uno sconto?	Can you give me a discount?
Ci devo pensare.	I have to think about it.

SMART TIPS

- Want to ask to see <u>this</u> shirt or <u>these</u> shoes? Here are the words you'll need to know:

	this		these	
m sing.	questo	m pl.	questi
m sing. (before vowel)	quest'		
f sing.	questa	f pl.	queste
f sing. (before vowel)	quest'		

- If you want to see <u>that</u> piece of jewelry or <u>those</u> flowers, these are the words you'll need:

	that		those	
m sing.	quel	m pl.	quei
m sing. (before s + consonant, z– or gn–)	quello	m pl.	quegli
m sing. (before vowel)	quell'	m pl.	quegli
f sing.	quella	f pl.	quelle
f sing. (before vowel)	quell'		

Activity A
Match the phrases below with the person who is speaking.

1 _____

2 _____

3 _____

?

4 _____

a Posso pagare con la carta di credito?

b Quanto costa?

c È troppo caro.

d Posso vedere quello?

Activity B
What do you say if…

1 …you want to try to get a discount?

_____

2 …you need to think about it?

_____

3 …you're just browsing?

_____

4 …you have only 20€?

_____

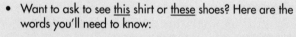

Regular *–ere* and *–ire* verbs in the present tense

To conjugate *–ere* verbs, remove the *–ere* ending and add the following endings.

	chiedere	**to ask**
(io)	chied**o**	I ask
(tu)	chied**i**	you ask
(Lei)	chied**e**	you ask
(lui/lei)	chied**e**	he/she asks
(noi)	chied**iamo**	we ask
(voi)	chied**ete**	you ask
(loro)	chied**ono**	they ask

To conjugate *–ire* verbs, remove the *–ire* ending and add the following endings.

	aprire	**to open**
(io)	apr**o**	I open
(tu)	apr**i**	you open
(Lei)	apr**e**	you open
(lui/lei)	apr**e**	he/she opens
(noi)	apr**iamo**	we open
(voi)	apr**ite**	you open
(loro)	apr**ono**	they open

Some *–ire* verbs follow a special pattern:

	finire	**to finish**
(io)	fin**isco**	I finish
(tu)	fin**isci**	you finish
(Lei)	fin**isce**	you finish
(lui/lei)	fin**isce**	he/she finishes
(noi)	fin**iamo**	we finish
(voi)	fin**ite**	you finish
(loro)	fin**iscono**	they finish

Other common verbs which follow the same pattern are *capire* (to understand), *preferire* (to prefer) and *spedire* (to send).

Here are some regular *–ere* and *–ire* verbs:

perdere	to lose
rispondere	to answer
scendere	to go down
vedere	to see
offrire	to offer
partire	to leave
sentire	to hear

Activity A
Conjugate the verb *partire*.

io _____

tu _____

Lei _____

lui/lei _____

noi _____

voi _____

loro _____

Activity B
Fill in the blanks with the correct conjugated verb.

1 Francesco _____ (*scendere*) dall'autobus.

2 (noi) _____ (*rispondere*) al telefono.

3 (voi) _____ (*finire*) il caffè.

4 (loro) _____ (*partire*) per Venezia.

Activity C
Match the Italian verbs to their English equivalents.

1 rispondere   a to go down

2 scendere   b to lose

3 perdere   c to answer

4 finire   d to finish

LESSON 5

La moda

DONNA — cappotto 45€, jeans 50€, borsa 60€, cintura 20€

UOMO — giubbino 75€, cravatta 20€, pantaloni 39€, camicia 30€

Fashion

Emilio needs to buy presents for his friends and they all want the latest fashion from Italy.

Activity A

Emilio only has 100€ to spend. Which combination of gifts can he buy?

a la cintura, la borsa, il giubbino

b il giubbino, i pantaloni, i jeans

c la camicia, il cappotto, la cravatta

Activity B

If you had 100€ to spend on gifts for yourself or others, what would you buy?

_____

_____

_____

Activity C

Write the total price of:

la borsa

i pantaloni

la camicia

la giacca sportiva

_____ €

SMART TIPS

• When Italians speak about clothes, they use the word *vestiti. Un vestito* can mean a piece of clothing, a dress (*vestito da donna*) or a suit (*vestito da uomo*).

• *Che taglia porta?* "What's your size?" Clothing and shoe sizes are different in Italy, so check the glossary for conversion charts.

Activity D

Find all the words from the image above in the word search.

```
R F C S C B H J Y D M K O P R P V X C C R A V A T T A A F G
C S S X V N J V D R M L O C M I A C S H K L N G F D C G R I
M R W A D G C E N J F I D X K L F N S J T D X M U O M O M U
S O D S B J K S B D S F H M X N K O T H K V N C C S X N J B
S Z D H U R U T S Z B J K L I Y R C X A C S G H K Y O P L B
A E F A E G Y I L I Y R D X W N K Y F S L T D Z V T W Q Z I
Z Q D C Q Z Q T E R G Y U F C Z V G Y H J O S B H U I I K N
T C S X R V B O D R S Z W A Q E Z D T N J K N O P L J G X O
A D A H F T E T U H F D O N N A T D S F H M B I S C G U I K
Q G Z P G N K U K L H Y T R D X V G F S A B H J K O L J U F
A B F Z P J I T K L T F D B O R S A S E W H N M K T E E W A
D G J A X O K Y I E S Z U O P R W Q V B N K L O T P W A D F
S B G T P A T H J L U H T F R E D A W C V B N M G H Y N W Q
S L O U O C P T E T F V B N C I N T U R A W S F G B H S J K
W A V G B N B K O U T E T H J K K L Y E W V N K L T E Q A F
```

LESSON 6

Words to Know

Core Words

l'abbigliamento	clothing
la bottiglia (di vino)	bottle (of wine)
la cartolina	postcard
i cosmetici	beauty products
il disegno	drawing
il gioiello	piece of jewelry
il giocattolo	toy
il libro	book
il maglione	sweater
il portachiavi	keychain
il profumo	perfume/cologne
il quadro	painting
la scatola di cioccolatini	box of chocolates
la sciarpa	scarf

Activity A

Complete the sentences with the correct souvenir.

1 Massimo vuole comprare un _____
in gioielleria.
piece of jewelry

2 Lorenzo vuole comprare un _____
per Sandro.
toy

3 Giorgia vuole comprare dei _____.
beauty products

4 Elena vuole comprare una _____
in tabaccheria.
post card

Activity B

Listen to what each person is looking for and label the correct item.

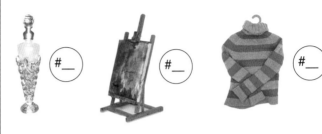

#___   #___   #___

Activity C

Match the Italian word to the English word.

1	il quadro	a	drawing
2	il giocattolo	b	scarf
3	il disegno	c	painting
4	la sciarpa	d	toy

Activity D

Make a list of the souvenirs you want to bring home for your friends and family.

SOUVENIR DA COMPRARE

_____
_____
_____
_____
_____
_____
_____
_____
_____

CULTURE TIP

IVA (*imposta sul valore aggiunto*) is the value-added tax that is included in all the prices you see in stores and restaurants. There is no additional tax—the price you see is the price you pay.

LESSON 7

Smart Phrases

CULTURE TIP

Make sure you check out the souvenirs of the different regions in Italy. For example, try the pottery in *Umbria* and leather goods in *Toscana*.

Core Phrases

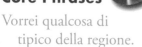

Vorrei qualcosa di tipico della regione.	I would like something typical from this region.
Le piace?	Do you like it?
Sì, mi piace.	Yes, I like it.
Lo può spedire/ incartare?	Can you ship/ wrap it?
Mi può fare un pacchetto regalo?	Can you gift-wrap it?
È un regalo.	It's a present.
Sono _____ euro.	The total is _____ euros.
Pago in contanti.	I'll pay in cash.
Il Suo resto.	Here is your change.

Activity B

How do you say…

1 …you want something from this region?

　　a Vorrei un pacchetto regalo.

　　b Vorrei qualcosa di tipico della regione.

2 …you will pay in cash?

　　a Pago con la carta di credito.

　　b Pago in contanti.

3 …it's for a present?

　　a È un regalo.

　　b Lo può spedire?

Activity A

Match the saleswoman's responses with Claudio's questions.

1　Posso pagare con la carta di credito?

2　Mi può fare un pacchetto?

3　Avete qualcosa di tipico della regione?

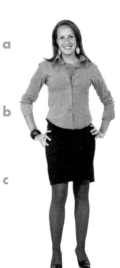

a　Sì, è un regalo?

b　Sì, certo. Abbiamo molti prodotti locali.

c　Accettiamo soltanto contanti.

Smart Grammar

Adjectives

grande	big
piccolo/piccola	small (m/f)
bello/bella	beautiful (m/f)
carino/carina	pretty (m/f)
brutto/brutta	ugly (m/f)
nuovo/nuova	new (m/f)
simpatico/simpatica	nice (m/f)
buono/buona	good (m/f)
cattivo/cattiva	bad (m/f)
caro/cara	expensive (m/f)
giovane	young
vecchio/vecchia	old (m/f)

I colori (Colors)

bianco/bianca	white (m/f)
nero/nera	black (m/f)
grigio/grigia	grey (m/f)
rosso/rossa	red (m/f)
arancione	orange
giallo/gialla	yellow (m/f)
verde	green
blu	blue
viola	purple
rosa	pink
marrone	brown

SMART TIP

The adjectives *blu* (blue), *viola* (purple) and *rosa* (pink) don't change form for gender or number. For example, *una sciarpa blu* (a blue scarf), *due vestiti blu* (two blue dresses) or *molte cravatte blu* (many blue ties.)

SMART TIPS

- In Italian, some adjectives go before nouns and some go after. The ones related to beauty, age, goodness and size most often go before the noun.

- Adjectives must always agree with the number and gender of the noun. For example, *due vecchi libri* or *due sciarpe rosse*. Note that *vecchi* (age) goes before the noun, but *rosse* (color) goes after it.

- *Bello* (beautiful) has the same forms as *quello*:

m sing.		bel	m pl.	bei
m sing. (before s + consonant, z– or gn–)		bello	m pl.	begli
m sing. (before vowel)		bell'	m pl.	begli
f sing.		bella	f pl.	belle
f sing. (before vowel)		bell'		

Activity A

Complete the sentences with the correct adjective.

1 Maria cerca un _____ quadro.
   beautiful

2 Questi profumi sono troppo _____.
   expensive

3 La T-shirt gialla è troppo _____.
   big

4 Questa sciarpa è _____.
   ugly

Activity B

Describe the articles of clothing below. Remember that the color goes after the noun.

1 _____   2 _____

3 _____   4 _____

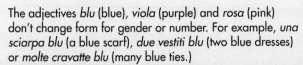

Activity A
Label the following stores.

1 _____   2 _____

3 _____   4 _____

Activity B
How do you ask…

1   …how much something costs?

_____

2   …to have something wrapped?

_____

3   …if you can get a discount?

_____

4   …where the cash register is?

_____

Challenge
Can you conjugate the following *–are*, *–ere* and *–ire* verbs?

1 *visitare* = to visit
2 *chiedere* = to ask
3 *capire* = to understand

Activity C
Choose the correct translation for the underlined word.

1   Marco cerca <u>un giocattolo</u>.
    a book   b toy

2   Aldo cerca <u>una cravatta</u>.
    a shirt   b tie

3   Luca cerca <u>un portachiavi</u>.
    a keychain   b bottle of wine

4   Cecilia cerca <u>un quadro</u>.
    a painting   b drawing

Activity D
Draw a picture of:

| 1 una piccola auto nera |
| 2 una grande bottiglia di vino rosso |
| 3 una bella borsa blu |

Internet Activity
Go online to **www.berlitzbooks.com/5Mtravel** to look at some of the latest fashion magazines in Italy. Print out a page and see if you can label all the articles of clothing!

Unit 8 **Technology**

In this unit you will learn how to:
- **talk about different kinds of technology.**
- **conjugate the verbs** *fare* **(to do, to make),** *dire* **(to say),** *scrivere* **(to write) and** *leggere* **(to read).**
- **use a computer and have a phone conversation.**

LESSON 1
La tecnologia

Dialogue

Robert has been in Italy for a few days and wants to find an internet café so that he can e-mail his family. Listen to his conversation with the hotel concierge.

Robert   Mi scusi, c'è un Internet Point qui vicino? Vorrei controllare la posta.

Portiere   Sì, c'è un Internet Point qui di fronte. Ma Lei ha un portatile?

Robert   Sì.

Portiere   Allora vada al bar in fondo alla strada: c'è il Wi-Fi gratuito.

Robert   Grazie mille!

CULTURE TIP

Several projects are running to offer free WiFi zones in Italy, especially in the larger cities. Most commonly you'll find Internet Points—storefronts where the use of computers and other technological services are offered.

SMART TIP

Qui means "here" and *lì* is "there." If you want to say "close to here" in Italian, say *qui vicino*, whereas *lì vicino* means "close to there." *Qui di fronte* means "across the way."

Activity A
Circle the correct answer.

1   Robert cerca _____.
   a un Internet Point   **b un computer**

2   C'è un Internet Point _____.
   a a sinistra dell'albergo   **b di fronte all'albergo**

3   Robert ha il suo _____.
   a portatile   **b cellulare**

4   Nel bar _____ c'è il Wi-Fi gratuito.
   a in fondo alla strada   **b dell'albergo**

Activity B
Listen to the dialogue again and fill in the missing words.

Robert   Mi scusi, c'è un _____ qui vicino? Vorrei controllare la posta.

Portiere   Sì, c'è un Internet Point qui _____. Ma Lei ha un _____?

Robert   Sì.

Portiere   Allora vada al bar _____ alla strada: c'è il Wi-Fi _____.

Robert   _____ mille!

Activity C
Answer the following questions in Italian.

1   Why is Robert looking for an Internet Point?
   _____

2   Is there an Internet Point near the hotel?
   _____

3   Why should Robert go to the café at the end of the street instead?
   _____

Words to Know

Core Words

l'adattatore	adapter (m)
il cellulare	cell phone [mobile]
la chiavetta USB	USB key/flash drive
il computer	computer
l'e-mail	e-mail (f)
Internet	Internet (m)
l'Internet Point	Internet Point
il mouse	mouse
il (computer) portatile	laptop
la tastiera	keyboard
lo schermo	screen
la stampante	printer
la tecnologia	technology
il Wi-Fi	WiFi

Extra Words

qui di fronte	across the way
in fondo a	at the end of

Activity A

Circle the best response.

1 Where do you go to check your e-mail?

 a l'Internet Point   **b il mouse**

2 What kind of computer can you carry around with you?

 a il cellulare   **b il portatile**

3 What do you use if your plug doesn't fit?

 a l'adattatore   **b lo schermo**

Activity B

Can you solve these riddles? Write the correct answers in Italian.

1 You can drag me around if you want to open a window.

 _____

2 I can write and draw but have no hands.

 _____

3 I can blink but have no eyes.

 _____

4 I have keys and locks but open no doors.

 _____

5 You can surf me but I have no waves.

 _____

Activity C

Label the following images.

1 _____   2 _____

3 _____   4 _____

CULTURE TIP

The Italian translation of "electronic mail" (the communication system) is *la posta elettronica*, and a single e-mail is *un messaggio di posta elettronica*. Too long? Many Italians would agree with you, and usually say *un'e-mail* or *un e-mail*: it can be either masculine or feminine. When plural, it's always feminine: *Devo leggere le e-mail*, "I have to read my e-mail."

Smart Phrases

Core Phrases

Devo mandare un'e-mail.	I need to send an e-mail.
Devo scaricare un documento.	I need to download a document.
Quanto costa collegarsi per 30 minuti/mezz'ora?	What is the price for 30 minutes of access?
C'è il Wi-Fi in albergo?	Do you have WiFi at this hotel?
Ci sono hotspot gratuiti?	Are there free hotspots?
Posso stampare la carta d'imbarco?	Can I print my boarding pass?

Activity A

What do you say if you want to…

1   …know if there are free hotspots?

   _____

2   …know how much 10 minutes of access costs?

   _____

3   …send an e-mail?

   _____

Activity B

Write the appropriate Italian questions to complete the conversation.

1   _____ ?   Trenta minuti sono 5€.

2   _____ ?   No, non abbiamo il Wi-Fi.

3   _____ ?   Sì, la può stampare qui.

4   _____ ?   Sì, c'è un hot spot in aeroporto.

LESSON 4

Smart Grammar

The verb *fare* (to do, to make)

The verb *fare* is irregular. The chart shows its conjugation in the present tense.

(io)	faccio	I do/make
(tu)	fai	you do/make
(Lei)	fa	you do/make
(lui/lei)	fa	he/she does/makes
(noi)	facciamo	we do/make
(voi)	fate	you do/make
(loro)	fanno	they do/make

While the verb *fare* is normally translated as "to do" or "to make," it can have different meanings when used with expressions such as:

fare attenzione	to pay attention
fare in fretta	to hurry
fare la fila	to stand in line
fare spese/shopping	to go shopping
fare sport	to play/practice sports
fare una passeggiata	to take a walk

Activity A

Fill in the blanks with the correct form of *fare*.

1 Gianni _____ le valigie.

2 (tu) _____ sport.

3 (voi) _____ in fretta, per favore!

4 Oggi non _____ freddo.

5 (io) _____ shopping con mia figlia.

6 (noi) _____ una passeggiata?

7 Non (loro) _____ mai attenzione.

Activity B

Circle the letter of the correct phrase.

1
   a Fa sport.
   b Fa una passeggiata.

2
   a Facciamo una passeggiata.
   b Facciamo la fila.

3
   a Faccio spese.
   b Faccio attenzione.

4
   a Fa le valigie.
   b Fa in fretta.

Activity C

How do you say...

1 ...the weather is nice?

   _____

2 ...it's cold out?

   _____

3 ...it's hot out?

   _____

4 ...the weather is bad?

   _____

LESSON 5

Il telefono

Bill has just bought a *carta telefonica* and is making a phone call from a payphone. Follow along with the instructions he sees on the phone.

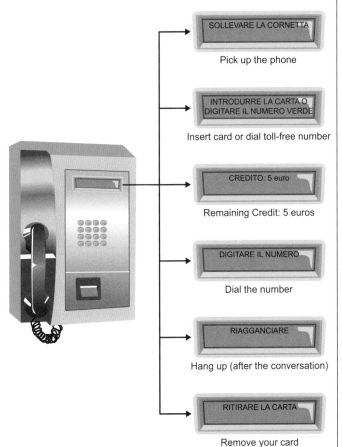

SOLLEVARE LA CORNETTA
Pick up the phone

INTRODURRE LA CARTA O DIGITARE IL NUMERO VERDE
Insert card or dial toll-free number

CREDITO: 5 euro
Remaining Credit: 5 euros

DIGITARE IL NUMERO
Dial the number

RIAGGANCIARE
Hang up (after the conversation)

RITIRARE LA CARTA
Remove your card

CULTURE TIP

If you're used to putting change in a pay phone to make a call, you'll notice that the phones in Italy are quite different. Very few phones accept coins: to make local calls, you usually need a calling card called *una carta telefonica*. Le carte telefoniche can be purchased at tobacco shops and post offices. If you plan on making international calls, a *carta telefonica internazionale* has much better international rates. Credits on a *carta telefonica* expire after two months.

Activity A

Circle **T** for true or **F** for false.

1   Calling cards in Italy can be bought in   **T / F**
    a *tabaccheria*.

2   Credits expire after four months.   **T / F**

3   A *carta telefonica* is best for making   **T / F**
    international calls.

4   A toll-free number is called a *numero verde*.   **T / F**

Activity B

Put the following steps in the correct order for making a phone call.

_____   Riagganciare

_____   Sollevare la cornetta

_____   Digitare il numero

_____   Ritirare la carta

_____   Introdurre la carta o digitare il numero verde

Activity C

What do you do when the phone indicates:

1   **sollevare la cornetta?**
    a Pick up the phone.
    b Hang up the phone.

2   **digitare il numero?**
    a Insert your card.
    b Dial the number.

3   **riagganciare?**
    a Pick up the phone.
    b Hang up the phone.

4   **ritirare la carta?**
    a Insert your card.
    b Remove your card.

SMART TIP

To make a call from Italy to the US, dial 00 + 1 + area code + phone number. To call the UK, dial 00 + 44 + area code + phone number.

Core Words

accendere	to turn on
aprire	to open
cliccare	to click
connettersi	to connect
eliminare	to delete
il file	file
inviare	to send
il link	link
nuovo messaggio	new message
la password	password
salvare	to save
scaricare	to download
scrivere	to write/to type
il sito	website
il software	software
spegnere	to turn off
stampare	to print

Activity A

Write the verb associated with each image.

1

_____

2

_____

3

_____

4

_____

Activity B

Complete the crossword puzzle.

Across

2 to print
5 to save

Down

1 website
3 to open
4 to send

Activity C

Circle the best response.

1 How do you open a new file?

  a file → aprire
  b file → nuovo messaggio

2 How do you delete a message?

  a eliminare
  b inviare

3 How do you turn on a computer?

  a accendere
  b spegnere

4 What do you click on to go to a website?

  a il link
  b la password

Smart Phrases

Core Phrases

Pronto?	Hello?
Chi parla?	Who's calling?
Sono ____.	It's ____ calling.
Potrei parlare con ____?	May I speak with ____?
Un momento.	One moment./Please hold.
Glielo/Gliela passo.	I'll get him/her.
Non c'è.	He/She is not here.
Vuole lasciare un messaggio?	Would you like to leave a message?
Gli/Le dica di richiamarmi, per favore.	Tell him/her to call me back, please.
Ha sbagliato numero.	You have the wrong number.

Activity A

Match the questions from column A with the correct responses in column B.

1 Vuole lasciare un messaggio?

2 Potrei parlare con Giulia?

3 Chi parla?

a Non c'è.

b Sono Vittoria.

c Gli dica di richiamarmi, per favore.

SMART TIP

Pronto is only used to say hello when you answer the phone. To say "hello" in person, say *buongiorno* during the day or *buonasera* in the evening.

Activity B

Sandro is calling to speak with Elena. Help him by completing the conversation.

Pronto? Chi parla?

_____

Buongiorno Sandro.

_____

Un momento. Gliela passo.

Activity C

How do you…

1 …introduce yourself on the phone?

_____

2 …say "you have the wrong number"?

_____

3 …say hello when you pick up the phone?

_____

4 …ask for someone to call you back?

_____

The verbs *dire* (to say), *scrivere* (to write) and *leggere* (to read)

The verb *dire* is irregular. The chart shows its conjugation in the present tense.

	dire	to say
(io)	dico	I say
(tu)	dici	you say
(Lei)	dice	you say
(lui/lei)	dice	he/she says
(noi)	diciamo	we say
(voi)	dite	you say
(loro)	dicono	they say

The verb *scrivere* is regular. The chart shows its conjugation in the present tense.

	scrivere	to write
(io)	scrivo	I write
(tu)	scrivi	you write
(Lei)	scrive	you write
(lui/lei)	scrive	he/she writes
(noi)	scriviamo	we write
(voi)	scrivete	you write
(loro)	scrivono	they write

The verb *leggere* is regular. The chart shows its conjugation in the present tense.

	leggere	to read
(io)	leggo	I read
(tu)	leggi	you read
(Lei)	legge	you read
(lui/lei)	legge	he/she reads
(noi)	leggiamo	we read
(voi)	leggete	you read
(loro)	leggono	they read

Activity A

Write the Italian equivalent next to the English phrase.

I write _____

you (sing., form.) read _____

she says _____

we write _____

you (pl.) read _____

they say _____

Activity B

Answer the following questions in Italian.

1   (Lei) Scrive ai Suoi amici (friends)?

_____

2   (Lei) Legge spesso (often) le e-mail?

_____

3   (Lei) Che cosa dice quando risponde al telefono?

_____

Activity C

Describe in Italian what each person is doing.

1

Giorgio _____.

2

Lucia _____.

3

Pronto?

Fabio _____.

Review

Activity A

How do you ask…

1 …if there is an internet café near your hotel?

_____

2 …if you can send an e-mail?

_____

3 …if you can print your boarding pass?

_____

4 …to speak with someone on the phone?

_____

Activity B

Complete the verb chart.

	scrivere	leggere
io		
tu		
Lei		
lui/lei		
noi		
voi		
loro		

Activity C

Match the Italian word in the left column to its English equivalent in the right column.

1	eliminare	a	to click
2	cliccare	b	to pick up the phone
3	sollevare la cornetta	c	to dial
4	accendere	d	to delete
5	digitare il numero	e	to turn on
6	riagganciare	f	to save
7	salvare	g	to hang up the phone

Activity D

Describe each picture in Italian.

1

(loro) _____

2

(lei) _____

3

(noi) _____

4

(io) _____

Challenge

Can you make up your own phone conversation in Italian? Pretend you're calling to talk to a friend and say the dialogue out loud.

Internet Activity

Want to practice typing *in italiano*? Go to **www.berlitzbooks.com/5Mtravel** for a list of websites that will help you learn how to type Italian accents or change your keyboard layout.

Unit 9 Nightlife

In this unit you will learn how to:
- talk about different nightlife options.
- use the prepositions *a* and *da*.
- strike up a conversation with a *stranger*.
- conjugate the verbs *uscire* (to go out) and *venire* (to come).

LESSON 1

Usciamo!

Dialogue

Alessio and Nadia are trying to figure out how to spend their first evening on vacation. Listen to their conversation.

Alessio	Che vuoi fare stasera?
Nadia	Voglio uscire!
Alessio	E dove vuoi andare?
Nadia	A ballare! Possiamo andare in discoteca.
Alessio	Sì, ma io non posso fare troppo tardi.

SMART TIPS

- *Troppo tardi* means "too late," but if you don't want to leave too early, use the word *presto*. For example, *Non voglio andare via troppo presto!* means "I don't want to leave too early!"
- *Stasera* means "this evening."

Activity A
Answer the following questions in Italian.

1 Che vuole fare Nadia stasera?

_____

2 Dove vuole andare?

_____

3 Alessio può fare molto tardi?

_____

Activity B
You are having a conversation with Alessio. Tell him what you want to do tonight.

Che vuoi fare stasera?

_____. Lei

Dove vuoi andare?

_____. Lei

Vuoi fare molto tardi?

_____. Lei

_____. Lei

CULTURE TIP

If you plan on staying out late, make sure you know how you're going to get home. Public transportation in most Italian cities runs until midnight, although sometimes there are night buses that run on a limited schedule. You can always ask where the nearest taxi stand is.

Words to Know

Core Words

il bar	bar
il bingo	bingo hall
il Casinò	casino
il cinema	movie theater
il concerto	concert
la discoteca	club
il jazz club	jazz club
il pub	pub
il teatro	theater [theatre]

Activity A

Choose the correct answer.

1 If you want to play poker, you should go to:

   a il Casinò   **b** il cinema

2 If you want to see a play by Pirandello, you should go to:

   a il concerto   **b** il teatro

3 If you want to listen to some relaxing music, you should go to:

   a il jazz club   **b** la discoteca

4 If you want to see a movie, you should go to:

   a il cinema   **b** il bingo

Activity B

List your three favorite places to go at night.

1 _____

2 _____

3 _____

Activity C

Listen to where each person wants to go this evening, and write the place in the blank.

1 Carlo vuole andare al _____.

2 Sofia vuole andare al _____.

3 Federico vuole andare al _____.

4 Alessia vuole andare in _____.

5 Matteo vuole andare al _____.

Activity D

Label the following places.

1 _____

2 _____

3 _____

4 _____

SMART PRONUNCIATION

Be sure to pronounce *Casinò* with the accent on the *o*. If you say it like the English word, it means "mess"!

Core Phrases

Mi piace…	I like…
la musica classica	classical music
la musica pop	pop music
il jazz	jazz
il rap	rap
il rock	rock music
l'opera	opera
Mi può consigliare un concerto?	Can you recommend a concert?
Quando inizia/finisce il concerto?	When does the concert begin/end?
Quanto (tempo) dura?	How long does it last?
Quanto costa il biglietto?	How much is a ticket?

CULTURE TIP

If you want to see a concert or play while you're in Italy, you can see schedules and buy tickets at the larger book/music/electronics stores such as *Feltrinelli* or on websites like TicketOne or Vivaticket.

Activity A

Say what kind of music each person likes.

1 A Renata piacciono Chopin, Beethoven e Cherubini.

_____

2 A Chiara e Alfredo piacciono Zucchero, Laura Pausini e Eros Ramazzotti.

_____

3 A me piacciono Louis Armstrong, Ella Fitzgerald e Dizzie Gillespie.

_____

Activity B

Fill in the blanks with the correct Italian word.

1 Quanto tempo _____?

2 Quanto _____ il biglietto?

3 Mi può _____ un concerto?

Activity C

Write the question associated with each answer.

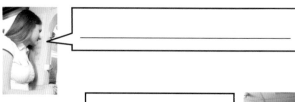

_____

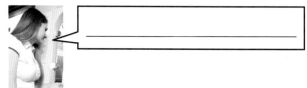
Il biglietto costa 35€.

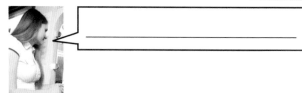

_____

Il concerto dura due ore.

_____

Il concerto finisce alle 23.

Smart Grammar

The prepositions *a* and *da*

In general, the preposition *a* means "to" and *da* means "from" when used before places and events. They often precede definite articles (*il, lo, la, l', i, gli, le*) and form contractions as follows:

	a	da
m sing.	a + il = al	da + il = dal
	a + lo = allo	da + lo = dallo
f sing.	a + la = alla	da + la = dalla
	a + l' = all'	da + l' = dall'
m pl.	a + i = ai	da + i = dai
	a + gli = agli	da + gli = dagli
f pl.	a + le = alle	da + le = dalle

For example:

Giorgio va alla festa.	Giorgio is going to the party.
Renata va al concerto.	Renata is going to the concert.
Alessandra viene dal cinema.	Alessandra is coming from the movie theater.
Martino ritorna dalle vacanze.	Martino is coming back from vacation [holiday].

> **SMART TIP**
>
> Don't forget to use the preposition *a* to talk about going to cities. For example, *In agosto vado a Firenze*, "I'm going to Florence in August."

Activity A

Choose the correct answer.

1 Andiamo _____ bar.

   a al   **b** dal

2 Vai _____ Torino?

   a a   **b** al

3 Venite _____ Firenze.

   a al   **b** da

> **SMART TIP**
>
> If you want to go to the *pizzeria* or *discoteca*, say *Voglio andare in pizzeria* and *Voglio andare <u>in</u> discoteca*.

Activity B

Complete the sentences with the correct preposition. Don't forget to use the correct contraction when necessary.

1 Tiziana va _____ museo.

2 Antonio e Laura ritornano in ufficio _____ ristorante.

3 Matteo va _____ Palermo.

4 Michela viene a casa _____ discoteca.

Activity C

Dove vuole andare? Write down 3 different places or monuments you want to visit. Make sure you use the correct preposition!

1 _____

2 _____

3 _____

Activity D

Write the correct contraction for:

1 a + il = _____

2 da + la = _____

3 a + le = _____

4 da + i = _____

5 a + la = _____

6 da + gli = _____

LESSON 5

Dove si va?

Where to go?

In many larger cities in Italy you can find weekly magazines that list all the concerts, movies and events for that week. Here's an example of the kinds of shows you might find.

Venerdì

h 20 – **Chopin, Preludi**
Sala Centrale, Auditorium, via del Fiume
35€

h 21 **Concerto Jazz**
Club La Palma, via Aliberti 13
Entrata libera

h 21.30 – **Concerto Rock**
Mondo Rock, piazza Santa Emerenziana
10€

h 22 **Serata di tango**
Club La Milonga, via del Gazometro 1
20€, 1 consumazione inclusa

Sabato

h 20.30 – **Vivaldi**, *Le quattro Stagioni*
Conservatorio Santa Cecilia, viale Manzoni
Entrata libera

h 21 ***Sei personaggi in cerca d'autore* di Luigi Pirandello**
Teatro Valle, via del Teatro Valle
25€

h 22 – **Serata hip-hop**
Magazzini Zeta, Molo 7
15€

Activity A

Fabio has had a long week and he needs to get out this weekend, but he only has 60€ to spend. He likes rock music, rap and classical plays. Where can he go, and how much money will he spend?

1 _____

2 _____

3 _____

Total: _____ €

Activity B

Which three activities/events would you choose?

1 _____

2 _____

3 _____

SMART TIP

If an event or museum is labeled *entrata libera*, it means that there is no charge for entry. You may still need a ticket, however, so make sure you check.

Activity C

Listen to each character and select the correct answer based on the events listed in the magazine.

1

a Il concerto è ai Magazzini Zeta.

b Il concerto è alle 21.30.

2

a Il concerto è al Club La Palma.

b Il concerto è al Teatro Valle.

3

a Il biglietto costa 25€.

b È alle 20.30.

Words to Know

Core Words

il bar	bar/cafè
il/la barman	bartender (m/f)
la bottiglia	bottle
il/la buttafuori	bouncer (m/f)
la consumazione	drink
il/la DJ	DJ (m/f)
il guardaroba	coat check
l'ingresso	cover charge
la pista da ballo	dance floor

CULTURE TIP

Many clubs in Italy offer you a drink with the cover charge. For example, you may see a sign: *Ingresso 20€, 1 consumazione inclusa* (Cover charge 20€, 1 free drink).

Activity A

Write in Italian where each person is.

1  _____

2 _____

3 _____

Activity B

Write the job of each person in Italian.

1   _____

2   _____

3  _____

Activity C

Choose the correct answer.

1 To check your coat, go to:
   a il buttafuori
   b il guardaroba

2 If you want a drink, go to:
   a il bar
   b la consumazione

3 If you want to dance, go to:
   a la pista da ballo
   b la bottiglia

4 When you enter the club you have to pay:
   a l'ingresso
   b il DJ

5 If you get a free drink with the cover charge, it's called a:
   a consumazione inclusa
   b consumazione d'ingresso

LESSON 7

Smart Phrases

Core Phrases

Le posso offrire un drink?	Can I buy you a drink?
Volentieri!	With pleasure!
Le va di ballare?	Do you want to dance?
È libero?	Is this seat free? (lit. "Is it free?")
Sì, è libero.	Yes, it's free.
Disturbo?	Am I interrupting?
Mi posso sedere?	Can I sit here?
Di che cosa si occupa?	What do you do for a living?
Lavoro alla _____.	I work for _____.
Studio.	I'm a student.
Sono in pensione.	I'm retired.

SMART TIP

If you're in a bar or club setting, people often use the informal *tu* instead of *Lei*. For example, someone might say *Ti posso offrire un drink?* or *Ti va di ballare?*

Activity A

Write three ways to strike up a conversation with a stranger.

1 _____

2 _____

3 _____

Activity B

How do you ask...

1 ...if the seat is taken?

_____

2 ...if you can join someone?

_____

3 ...if you're interrupting?

_____

4 ...if you can buy someone a drink?

_____

Activity C

Write the logical question for each answer.

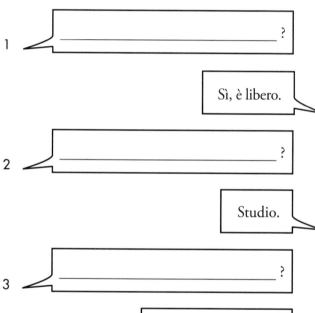

1 _____ ?

Sì, è libero.

2 _____ ?

Studio.

3 _____ ?

Sì, mi va di ballare!

4 _____ ?

Volentieri!

The verbs *uscire* (to go out) and *venire* (to come)

The verb *uscire* (to go out) is irregular in the present tense.

	uscire	to go out
(io)	esco	I go out
(tu)	esci	you go out
(Lei)	esce	you go out
(lui/lei)	esce	he/she goes out
(noi)	usciamo	we go out
(voi)	uscite	you go out
(loro)	escono	they go out

The verb *venire* (to come) is irregular in the present tense.

	venire	to come
(io)	vengo	I come
(tu)	vieni	you come
(Lei)	viene	you come
(lui/lei)	viene	he/she comes
(noi)	veniamo	we come
(voi)	venite	you come
(loro)	vengono	they come

Activity A

Fill in the blanks with the correct form of the verb *venire*.

1 (voi) _____ al cinema o andate al teatro?

2 Stasera (io) _____ con voi a mangiare una pizza.

3 (tu) _____ al concerto o rimani a casa?

4 (loro) _____ in discoteca?

5 (tu) _____ questo weekend.

6 (Lei) _____ con i Suoi amici?

7 (lei) _____ al cinema con noi.

Activity B

Fill in the blanks with the correct form of the verb *uscire*.

1 Stasera (tu) _____ con Francesco.

2 (loro) _____ dalla discoteca con Marco.

3 A che ora (Lei) _____?

4 Stasera (noi) _____?

5 (io) _____ alle 9.

6 (noi) _____ insieme (together).

7 (lui) _____ dal cinema con Alessandra.

Activity C

Answer the questions in Italian.

1 Con chi uscite?

_____

2 A che ora vengono?

_____

3 Esci con noi?

_____

4 Viene anche Marina?

_____

Activity D

Choose the correct answer.

1 _____ in vacanza con voi.

   a Veniamo   b Usciamo

2 _____ di casa alle 8.

   a Viene   b Esce

3 Domani non (io) _____ al cinema.

   a vengo   b esco

4 _____ in discoteca.

   a Vengono   b Escono

SMART TIP

The verbs *rimanere* (to stay) and *salire* (to go up) follow the same pattern as *venire*: *rimango, rimani*, etc., and *salgo, sali*, etc. For example, *Rimango fino alle 2* "I'll stay until 2," and *Sale sull'autobus* "He/She gets on the bus."

Activity A

List three different places where you can go at night.

1 _____

2 _____

3 _____

Activity B

Select the correct preposition for each sentence.

1 Dario va _____ concerto jazz.

   a al   **b** alla

2 Sandra va _____ Milano.

   a alla   **b** a

3 Tiziana ritorna _____ cinema.

   a dal   **b** da

Activity C

Complete the crossword puzzle.

Across

2 club
6 bouncer
8 from
9 bottle

Down

1 theater
3 coat check
4 bartender
5 dance floor
7 to go out

Activity D

Select the logical answer for each question.

1 Quanto tempo dura?

   a Due ore e mezzo.

   b Mi piace l'opera.

2 Le va di ballare?

   a Volentieri!

   b Sono in pensione.

3 Quanto costa il biglietto?

   a Alle 21.30.

   b 20€.

Activity E

Complete the verb charts.

	uscire	venire
io		
tu		
Lei		
lui/lei		
noi		
voi		
loro		

Challenge

Can you conjugate the verb *uscire* out loud without writing it down?

Internet Activity

Want to see what's happening in Rome this week? How about Florence or Naples? Go online to **www.berlitzbooks.com/5Mtravel** to find links to Italian websites where you can look for events that interest you.

In this unit you will learn:
- how to ask for help.
- what to say at the doctor's office.
- different parts of the body.
- reflexive verbs and the past tense with *avere*.

LESSON 1

Aiuto!

Dialogue

It's *23h00* and Anne is looking for an all-night pharmacy. She has just stopped a passing *poliziotto* (police officer) to ask for help.

Anne	Mi scusi. Mi può aiutare per favore?
Poliziotto	Certo, Signora.
Anne	Cerco la farmacia notturna.
Poliziotto	Non è lontano.
Anne	Mi può indicare la strada?
Poliziotto	Prenda la seconda strada a destra, la farmacia è sulla Sua sinistra.
Anne	Grazie mille!
Poliziotto	Di niente.

Activity A

Circle **T** for True and **F** for False.

1	Anne cerca una farmacia.	T / F
2	Anne parla con un poliziotto.	T / F
3	La farmacia è aperta tutta la notte.	T / F
4	La farmacia è lontano.	T / F

SMART TIP

Something that is open or runs all night is *notturno/notturna*. Other examples include *servizio notturno* (all-night service) and *autobus notturno* (night bus).

Activity B

Imagine you are looking for an all-night pharmacy. Complete the conversation with the police officer.

La posso aiutare?

_____ Lei

Non è lontano.

_____ Lei

Prenda la seconda strada a destra, la farmacia è sulla Sua sinistra.

_____ Lei

LESSON 2

Words to Know

Core Words

il commissariato	police station
la farmacia	pharmacy
la farmacia notturna	all-night pharmacy
il/la farmacista	pharmacist (m/f)
l'infermiere/l'infermiera	nurse (m/f)
il medico	doctor
l'ospedale	hospital (m)
la polizia	police
il poliziotto, il carabiniere	police officer
il pronto soccorso	emergency room [casualty department]
lo studio medico	doctor's office
il vigile del fuoco	firefighter

CULTURE TIPS

- There are various police forces in Italy. *La Polizia* is the national police force, and *i Carabinieri* are a special branch of the army with similar functions to the police.

- If you need to call for help in Italy, dial 118 for medical, 112 for *Carabinieri*, 113 for police and 115 for fire. Note that often firefighters respond to medical emergencies.

Activity A

Write who to call along with the phone number if there is a...

1 ...fire.

_____ (_____)

2 ...medical emergency.

_____ (_____)

3 ...theft.

_____ (_____)

Activity B

Label each person.

1 _____ 2 _____

3 _____ 4 _____

Activity C

Label each place.

 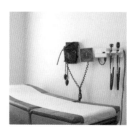

1 _____ 2 _____

3 _____

Smart Phrases

Core Phrases

Al fuoco!	Fire!
Aiuto!	Help!
Al ladro!	Thief!
Attenzione!	Watch out!
Mi hanno scippato/ scippata!	I've been robbed! (m/f)
Mi sono rotto/rotta il braccio/la gamba.	I (m/f) broke my arm/my leg.
Sono…	I am…
asmatico/asmatica	asthmatic (m/f)
diabetico/diabetica	diabetic (m/f)
malato/malata	sick (m/f)

Activity A
What should you say if…

1 …you are robbed?

_____

2 …there is a fire?

_____

3 …you need help?

_____

4 …someone is going to trip and fall?

_____

5 …you broke your leg?

_____

6 …you are diabetic?

_____

Activity B
Write what each person would say to describe his or her ailment.

1 _____

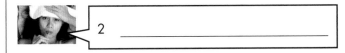

2 _____

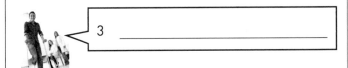

3 _____

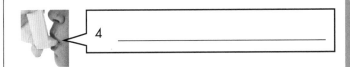

4 _____

Activity C
Unscramble the letters and write the correct phrases.

1 u t o a i   _ _ _ _ _

2 c l o a f o u   _ _ _ _ _ _ _

3 n a e i t n e z o t _ _ _ _ _ _ _ _ _ _

4 a o d l a r l   _ _ _ _ _ _ _

Activity D
Match the English expressions with their Italian equivalents.

1 Fire!   a Attenzione!

2 Watch out!   b Al ladro!

3 Help!   c Al fuoco!

4 Thief!   d Aiuto!

LESSON 4
Smart Grammar

Reflexive Verbs

Reflexive verbs are used when the subject is performing the action on himself, herself or itself. They take two steps to conjugate. First, you must use the correct reflexive pronoun and then you must conjugate the verb following regular conjugation patterns. For example, take the reflexive verb *sentirsi* (to feel).

(io)	**mi**	sento	I feel
(tu)	**ti**	senti	you feel
(Lei)	**si**	sente	you feel
(lui/lei)	**si**	sente	he/she feels
(noi)	**ci**	sentiamo	we feel
(voi)	**vi**	sentite	you feel
(loro)	**si**	sentono	they feel

Here are some other reflexive verbs (note that the infinitive uses *si*):

addormentarsi	to fall asleep
alzarsi	to get up
chiamarsi	to call oneself/to be named
divertirsi	to enjoy oneself
farsi la barba	to shave
farsi la doccia	to take a shower
lavarsi	to wash oneself
lavarsi le mani/ i denti/i capelli	to wash (one's hands/ teeth/hair)
riposarsi	to rest
rompersi (il braccio/ la gamba)	to break (one's arm/leg)
svegliarsi	to wake up
vestirsi	to get dressed

SMART TIP

The reflexive pronoun used for *Lei* (you form.) used to be capitalized. For example: *A che ora Si alza?* (What time do you wake up?) It's not done anymore in modern Italian, but you can still find the capitalized *Si* in formal and official texts.

SMART TIP

To say that you feel sick in Italian, you can say either *Mi sento male* (I feel bad/sick) or *Non mi sento bene* (I don't feel well).

Activity A
Fill in the blanks with the correct reflexive pronoun.

1 (lui) _____ chiama Giacomo.

2 (noi) _____ alziamo alle 7.

3 (tu) _____ fai la barba?

4 (Lei) _____ riposa.

Activity B
Write what is happening in each picture.

1 Giorgio _____.

2 Anna _____.

3 Lui _____.

Activity C
Match the personal pronoun with the correct reflexive pronoun.

1	io	a	ci
2	noi	b	ti
3	loro	c	si
4	voi	d	Si
5	tu	e	mi
6	Lei	f	vi

LESSON 5

La salute

Dialogue

Jim has a *febbre* (fever) and is feeling *male* (bad) while on vacation. Listen to his conversation with *il medico* (the doctor).

Jim	Dottore, non mi sento bene.
Il medico	Che sintomi ha?
Jim	Ho la febbre e il mal di testa.
Il medico	Ha anche la tosse?
Jim	Sì, e mi fa male la gola.
Il medico	È l'influenza.
Jim	Che cosa mi consiglia di fare?
Il medico	Si deve riposare e deve bere molta acqua.

SMART TIPS

- If something hurts you, say *Mi fa male* followed by the body part that hurts. For example, *Mi fa male la gola* means "My throat hurts."

- For some body parts you can also say *Ho mal di...* For example: *Ho mal di testa* (head)/*gola* (throat)/*stomaco* (stomach)/*schiena* (back).

Activity A

Circle **T** for True and **F** for False.

1	Jim si sente male.	**T / F**
2	Il medico dice che ha l'influenza.	**T / F**
3	Jim si deve riposare.	**T / F**
4	Jim deve bere molto vino.	**T / F**

CULTURE TIP

At public hospitals in Italy, patients may receive emergency services at no cost or upon payment of a limited contribution. Non-emergency services provided by public hospitals are subject to a fee.

Activity B

Check off Jim's symptoms.

☐	Ha mal di stomaco.
☐	Ha la tosse.
☐	Ha mal di testa.
☐	Vomita.
☐	Ha la febbre.

Activity C

How do you say…

1 …you have a headache?

_____

2 …you feel sick?

_____

3 …you have the flu?

_____

4 …you have a sore throat?

_____

Your Turn

Imagine that you're at a doctor's office with the flu. Practice describing your symptoms to the doctor.

LESSON 6
Words to Know

Core Words

Il corpo (Body)

il braccio/le braccia	arm/arms
il dito/le dita	finger/fingers
la gamba	leg
il ginocchio/le ginocchia	knee/knees
la gola	throat
la mano/le mani	hand/hands
il petto	chest
il piede	foot
la schiena	back
la spalla	shoulder
lo stomaco	stomach
la testa	head

Il viso (Face)

la bocca	mouth
i capelli	hair
il dente	tooth
la lingua	tongue
il naso	nose
l'occhio	eye
l'orecchio/le orecchie	ear/ears

SMART TIPS

- Some body parts change gender from singular to plural. For example, "arm" changes from masculine in the singular to feminine in the plural: *il braccio/le braccia*.

- *Capelli* is plural in Italian. The singular, *un capello*, means just one strand of hair. Make sure you use a plural adjective when describing hair. For example, *Ha i capelli biondi*, "He has blond hair."

Activity A
Label the parts of the face in Italian.

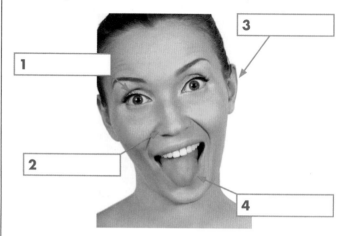

1 _____
2 _____
3 _____
4 _____

Activity B
Label the parts of the body in Italian.

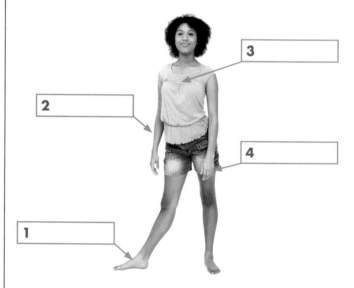

1 _____
2 _____
3 _____
4 _____

Activity C
Complete the word webs with parts of *il corpo* or *il viso*.

il corpo

il viso

Smart Phrases

Core Phrases

Vorrei…	I would like…
un antiacido	antacids
una confezione di aspirina	aspirin
dei cerotti	bandages [plasters]
un filtro solare	sunscreen
una confezione di paracetamolo	acetaminophen [paracetamol]
delle pasticche per la gola	throat lozenges
uno sciroppo per la tosse	cough syrup

Che cosa mi consiglia per…?	What do you recommend for…?
l'influenza	the flu
il mal d'auto	motion sickness
il mal di stomaco	stomach pains
la nausea	nausea
la tosse	a cough
il raffreddore	a cold
l'indigestione	indigestion

Deve avere la ricetta.	You need a prescription.

CULTURE TIP

Pharmacies are easy to spot in Italy; they all display a green cross outside, which is often lit by neon. If you need a pharmacy, just follow the flashing green lights.

Activity A

Circle the items that can be purchased at *la farmacia*.

pane
pasticche per la tosse
cerotti
gelati
antiacido
aspirina
biglietti

Activity B

Write the medicine that each person needs.

1 Nicoletta ha mal di gola.

_____

2 Davide ha mal di testa.

_____

3 Sandra ha la tosse.

_____

Activity C

How do you ask what the pharmacist recommends for…

1 …nausea?

_____

2 …a cold?

_____

3 …motion sickness?

_____

LESSON 8

Smart Grammar

Past tense using *avere*

To form the past tense—or *passato prossimo*—of most verbs, use the present tense of *avere* before the past participle of the main verb.

Regular *–are* verbs

To form the past participle of regular *–are* verbs, drop the *–are* ending and add *–ato*.

		viaggiare	**to travel**
(io)	ho	viaggiato	I travelled
(tu)	hai	viaggiato	you travelled
(Lei)	ha	viaggiato	you travelled
(lui/lei)	ha	viaggiato	he/she travelled
(noi)	abbiamo	viaggiato	we travelled
(voi)	avete	viaggiato	you travelled
(loro)	hanno	viaggiato	they travelled

Regular *–ere* verbs

To form the past participle of regular *–ere* verbs, drop the *–ere* ending and add *–uto*. Here, an *i* is also added for pronunciation purposes.

		conoscere	**to meet**
(io)	ho	conosciuto	I met
(tu)	hai	conosciuto	you met
(Lei)	ha	conosciuto	you met
(lui/lei)	ha	conosciuto	he/she met
(noi)	abbiamo	conosciuto	we met
(voi)	avete	conosciuto	you met
(loro)	hanno	conosciuto	they met

Regular *–ire* verbs

To form the past participle of regular *–ire* verbs, drop the *–ire* ending and add *–ito*.

		domire	**to sleep**
(io)	ho	dormito	I slept
(tu)	hai	dormito	you slept
(Lei)	ha	dormito	you slept
(lui/lei)	ha	dormito	he/she slept
(noi)	abbiamo	dormito	we slept
(voi)	avete	dormito	you slept
(loro)	hanno	dormito	they slept

SMART TIPS

- To use the negative in the past tense, place the *non* before the conjugated verb *avere*. For example, *Non ho trovato la farmacia*, "I didn't find the pharmacy."
- Some of the verbs you have already learned have irregular past participles:

aprire → aperto	prendere → preso
bere → bevuto	rispondere → risposto
chiedere → chiesto	scrivere → scritto
chiudere → chiuso	scegliere → scelto
fare → fatto	vedere → visto
leggere → letto	

Activity A

Write the correct past participle for each verb.

mangiare	
riuscire	
vendere	
bere	
rispondere	
viaggiare	
scrivere	
fare	
pagare	

Activity B

Answer the following questions in the past tense.

1   Ha visto il Colosseo?

_____

2   Ha scelto la pizza?

_____

3   Ha risposto al telefono?

_____

4   Ha comprato un vestito?

_____

5   Ha fatto le valigie?

_____

Activity A

How do you say…

1 …someone stole your wallet?

_____

2 …"Help!"?

_____

3 …you broke your leg?

_____

4 …your feet hurt?

_____

5 …your throat hurts?

_____

Activity B

Describe each person.

1 Massimo _____.

2 Lucia _____.

3 Matteo _____.

4 Alice _____.

Activity C

Check off symptoms of *l'influenza*.

☐ Mi fa male la testa.

☐ Ho la febbre.

☐ Mi fa male un ginocchio.

☐ Ho mal di gola.

☐ Ho il mal d'auto.

☐ Ho la tosse.

Activity D

Put the following sentences in the *passato prossimo*.

1 Viaggio con la mia famiglia.

_____

2 Scegliamo un primo e un secondo.

_____

3 Anna e Luisa mangiano un gelato.

_____

4 Giorgio non risponde al cellulare.

_____

5 Guardi la televisione.

_____

Challenge

Stand in front of a mirror and point to and name at least 10 parts of your body or face.

Internet Activity

Go online to **www.berlitzbooks.com/5Mtravel** to find tips on how to have a safe trip in Italy and then make a list of 5 things you can do to keep safe.

Unit 11 Heading Home

In this unit you will learn how to:
- talk about family members.
- use comparatives.
- describe your trip.
- form the past tense using *essere*.

LESSON 1

Cari amici

A Postcard

Ryan is at the end of his trip and wants to *mandare* (send) some postcards to his *amici* (friends) at home who are learning Italian. Read his message to Susan and answer the questions that follow.

Cara Susan,

Roma è una bella città, ci sono molte cose da fare e io mi diverto. Ho visitato il Colosseo, la Fontana di Trevi e il Vaticano. Ci sono dei buoni ristoranti e io ho mangiato molto! Ma ho anche parlato italiano con molte persone.

A presto,
Ryan

Susan Jones
305 Oak Street
Princeton, NJ 08540
Stati Uniti

Activity B

Ryan leaves tomorrow. Check off what he's done already to find out what he still needs to do today.

DA FARE

_____ visitare il Colosseo

_____ andare al museo

_____ parlare con le persone

_____ mangiare molto

_____ vedere uno spettacolo

_____ visitare il Vaticano

Activity C

Practice writing your own postcard.

Activity A

Fill in the missing words from Ryan's postcard.

1 A Roma _____ molte cose da fare.

2 Io mi _____.

3 Ho _____ il Colosseo, la Fontana di Trevi e il Vaticano.

4 Ci sono dei _____.

5 (io) _____ con molte persone.

SMART TIP

A typical greeting for letters and postcards is *Caro* (m), *Cara* (f), *Cari* (m pl.) or *Care* (f pl.), which all mean "Dear...."

CULTURE TIP

Don't forget that stamps can be bought at the post office and at *tabaccherie*. Once your postcard is ready to go, drop it at the post office or in one of the red mailboxes you can find on the street. In larger cities, there will be one slot for local mail and another slot labeled *Per tutte le altre destinazioni* (For all other destinations).

Words to Know

Core Words

la famiglia	family
il marito	husband
la moglie	wife
il compagno/la compagna	partner (m/f)
i figli	children
il figlio	son
la figlia	daughter
i genitori	parents
il padre	father
la madre	mother
il fratello	brother
la sorella	sister
il nonno	grandfather
la nonna	grandmother
il/la nipote	grandson/grandaughter; nephew/niece (m/f)
il cugino/la cugina	cousin (m/f)
lo zio	uncle
la zia	aunt

Activity A

Choose the correct picture for each underlined phrase.

1 Teresa vuole comprare una camicia per <u>suo padre</u>.

2 Luca vuole mandare una cartolina a <u>suo figlio</u>.

3 Lorenzo vuole partire con <u>sua sorella</u>.

4 Silvia e Gianni vogliono comprare un souvenir per <u>la loro nonna</u>.

Activity B

Don't forget to bring home some souvenirs! Write what you want to buy for each of the following people:

1 i miei genitori _____

2 i miei figli _____

3 mio zio _____

4 mia cugina _____

5 il mio compagno/ _____
   la mia compagna

Core Phrases

A presto, spero!	Hope to see you soon.
Alla prossima!	See you next time!
È stato un piacere.	It was a pleasure.
Mi sono divertito/divertita.	I had a great time. (m/f)
Grazie della cortesia/ dell'ospitalità.	Thank you for your kindness/hospitality.
Rimaniamo in contatto.	Let's keep in touch.
Mi mancherai.	I'm going to miss you.
Ci vediamo!	See you soon!

SMART TIP

To say, "I'll miss you" in Italian, you actually say "You'll be missing to me," (*Tu*) *mi mancherai.*

Activity A

How do you say…

1   …you want to keep in touch?

_____

2   …you had a great time?

_____

3   …you're going to miss the other person?

_____

4   …you hope to see the other person soon?

_____

5   …it was a pleasure?

_____

Activity B

Fill in the missing words from the phrases and arrange the circled letters to find a bonus word.

1   A ___ ___◯___ ___ ___, spero!

2   Alla ◯___ ___ ___ ___ ___ ___ ___.

3   È stato un ___ ___ ___ ___ ___◯___.

4   Mi sono ◯___ ___ ___ ___ ___ ___ ___ ___.

5   Rimaniamo in ___ ___ ___ ___◯___ ___ ___.

Bonus word: ___ ___ ___ ___ ___

Activity C

Write the Italian equivalent of each phrase.

1

See you next time!

2

It was a pleasure.

3

I'm going to miss you.

…

SMART TIPS

- If something is better or worse, use the comparatives *migliore* (better) and *peggiore* (worse). For example, *L'albergo a quattro stelle* (stars) *è migliore dell'albergo a due stelle*, "The four-star hotel is better than the two-star hotel."

- Make sure that the adjective agrees with the first noun. For example, *Anna è più alta di suo fratello*, "Anna is taller than her brother."

- In superiority and inferiority comparatives, if the second term is preceded by a preposition, use *che* istead of *di*. For example, *In Italia ci sono più cellulari che in Francia*, "In Italy there are more cell phones than in France."

I comparativi (Comparatives)

There are three ways to form comparatives in Italian when used with adjectives:

Superiority: più... di

Roma è più grande
di Firenze.

Rome is bigger
than Florence.

Inferiority: meno... di

Il treno è meno veloce
dell'aereo.

The train is slower than
the plane. (Literally,
The train is less fast
than the plane.)

Equality: ... come

Mio fratello è alto
come mio padre.

My brother is as tall as
my father.

Activity A

Use the words below to create your own comparative sentences.

1   mio padre, mia madre

   _____

2   l'italiano, l'inglese

   _____

3   il dolce, l'insalata

   _____

4   il vino, la birra

   _____

5   mia nonna, mia madre

   _____

Activity B

Compare the following people and items.

1

Matteo   Mattia

Mattia è _____ alto di Matteo.

2

La camicia è cara _____ le scarpe.

3

| Roma | 20°C |
| ■ Napoli | 25°C |

A Roma fa _____ caldo che a Napoli.

Activity C

Choose the logical comparative for the following sentences.

1   Roma è _____ grande di Venezia.

2   L'insalata è _____ cara della bistecca.

3   Fa _____ caldo in Egitto che in Russia.

4   Mia nonna è _____ giovane di mia madre.

5   Il ristorante a tre stelle è _____ del ristorante a due stelle.

Arrivederci!

Dialogue

Ryan has just finished packing his bags and he's saying goodbye to his colleague, Lucio.

Lucio	Ha fatto le valigie?
Ryan	Sì, parto oggi: ritorno a casa.
Lucio	Le è piaciuta la città?
Ryan	Mi è piaciuta molto. Da noi non ci sono città così belle!
Lucio	Ha visitato molti monumenti?
Ryan	Sì e ho anche comprato molti souvenir per la mia famiglia.
Lucio	È stato un piacere conoscerla.
Ryan	Anche per me! A presto, spero!

SMART TIPS

- To say that you liked something, say *mi è piaciuto/ piaciuta*, depending on if the thing you liked is masculine or feminine. The plural forms are *mi sono piaciuti/ piaciute*. *La città mi è piaciuta*, for example, means "I liked the city."

- The preposition *da* has many different meanings. When used in the expression *da me/da noi*, it can mean "at my/our house" or "where I'm/we are from." If you're sick, you can go *dal medico*, "to the doctor's."

Activity A

Circle **T** for true or **F** for false.

1 Lucio ha fatto le valigie.   **T / F**
2 Ryan non parte oggi.   **T / F**
3 A Ryan è piaciuta molto la città.   **T / F**
4 Ryan ha visitato molti monumenti.   **T / F**

Activity B

Imagine you are saying goodbye to Lucio. Complete the dialogue.

Ha fatto le valigie?

Le è piaciuta la città?

Ha visitato molti monumenti?

È stato un piacere conoscerla.

Activity C

Answer the questions based on the dialogue in Italian.

1 Ryan ha fatto le valigie?

_____

2 A Ryan è piaciuta la città?

_____

3 Ryan ha visitato molti monumenti?

_____

4 Ryan ha comprato dei souvenir?

_____

Core Words

divertente	fun
fantastico/fantastica	fantastic [brilliant] (m/f)
incredibile	incredible
interessante	interesting
magnifico/magnifica	magnificent (m/f)
noioso/noiosa	boring (m/f)
orribile	horrible
pessimo/pessima	awful, dreadful (m/f)
romantico/romantica	romantic (m/f)
squisito/squisita	delicious (m/f)
simpatico/simpatica	nice (m/f)
strano/strana	strange (m/f)

SMART TIP

When describing how something was in the past, Italian often uses the imperfect tense of *essere*. For example, *Il film era noioso*, "The film was boring," or *I souvenir erano cari*, "The souvenirs were expensive."

Activity A

Write 5 sentences to describe a current or past vacation [holiday].

1 _____

2 _____

3 _____

4 _____

5 _____

Activity B

Fill in the blanks with the correct adjective. Make sure it agrees with the noun!

1   Il film era _____.
                    interesting

2   Il concerto era _____.
                        boring

3   La città è molto _____.
                          romantic

4   I letti dell'albergo erano _____.
                                    awful

5   Il museo è _____.
                    magnificent

Activity C

List four *buoni* (good) adjectives and four *cattivi* (bad).

buoni

cattivi

Your Turn

Use your new vocabulary to describe your best vacation ever and your worst vacation ever.

Smart Phrases

Core Phrases

Sono andato/andata in Italia.	I went to Italy. (m/f)
È stato il miglior viaggio della mia vita!	It was the best trip of my life!
Sono stati tutti molto gentili.	Everyone was very nice.
Ho conosciuto molte persone.	I met a lot of people.
Non vedo l'ora di…	I can't wait to…
partire	leave
rientrare	go home
ritornare	go back
vedere le foto	see the pictures
rivederla	see you again
Voglio rimanere.	I want to stay longer.
Mi sono proprio divertito/divertita.	I had a great time. (m/f)
Sono rimasto/rimasta ____ giorni/settimane/mesi.	I stayed there for ____ days/weeks/months. (m/f)

Activity A

How do you say…

1 …you stayed there for 6 days?

_____

2 …you went to Italy?

_____

3 …you can't wait to see the pictures?

_____

4 …you can't wait to go back?

_____

Activity B

Did these people have a good time on their vacation?

1

Non vedo l'ora di ritornare!

a Si è divertito.
b Non si è divertito.

2

Non vedo l'ora di rientrare.

a Si è divertita.
b Non si è divertita.

3

Vogliamo rimanere!

a Si sono divertiti.
b Non si sono divertiti.

Activity C

Answer the questions in Italian.

1 (Lei) È andato/andata in Italia?

_____

2 Ha conosciuto molte persone?

_____

3 Sono stati tutti molto gentili?

_____

> **SMART TIP**
>
> *Ci* means "there" when used to replace locations. For example, *Ci vado* means "I'm going there." *Non vedo l'ora di andarci* means "I can't wait to go there." In this case *–ci* is added to the end of the infinitive.

The past tense using *essere*

You already learned how to form the *passato prossimo* with *avere*. Some verbs form the *passato prossimo* with *essere*. For example:

È arrivato in ritardo.   He arrived late.

Here is a list of verbs that use *essere* in the *passato prossimo*. Most verbs of motion and all reflexive verbs take *essere* in the *passato prossimo* (e.g., *divertirsi, vestirsi, farsi la doccia*).

andare → andato/andata	to go
arrivare → arrivato/arrivata	to arrive
cadere → caduto/caduta	to fall
entrare → entrato/entrata	to enter
morire → morto/morta	to die
nascere → nato/nata	to be born
partire → partito/partita	to leave
passare → passato/passata	to pass
rimanere → rimasto/rimasta	to stay
ritornare → ritornato/ritornata	to return
salire → salito/salita	to go up, to climb
scendere → sceso/scesa	to go down, to descend
uscire → uscito/uscita	to go out
venire → venuto/venuta	to come

For all verbs that take *essere*, the past participle must agree with the subject in gender and number. For example:

È <u>andato</u> in Italia.   He went to Italy.
Si è <u>vestita</u>.   She got dressed.
Si sono <u>vestiti</u>.   They (m) got dressed.
Sono <u>andate</u> in Italia.   They (f) went to Italy.

Activity A
Write the following sentences in the *passato prossimo*.

1   (loro, f) Rimangono tre giorni a Pisa.

_____

2   (lei) Arriva alle 3 di notte.

_____

3   (lui) Si diverte.

_____

4   (io, m) Vengo con la mia famiglia.

_____

5   (noi, f) Andiamo all'aeroporto.

_____

Activity B
Fill in the blanks with the correct form of *avere* or *essere*.

1   Giulio _____ caduto dalla scala.
2   (loro) _____ andate in vacanza.
3   Marta _____ mangiato una pizza.
4   (noi) _____ fatto le valigie.
5   (voi) _____ saliti in camera.

Activity C
Write the correct past participle for each verb.

venire	
andare	
rimanere	
arrivare	
uscire	
nascere	
passare	
scendere	
cadere	

Activity A

Write a postcard to an Italian friend telling him or her about your recent vacation.

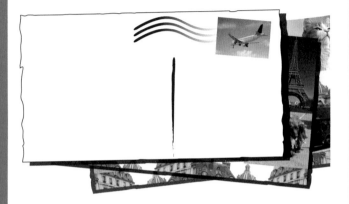

Activity B

Compare the people in the following pictures.

Laura   Carlo

1   Carlo è _____ di Laura.

La principessa

La strega

2   La strega è _____ della principessa.

Marco   Silvia

3   Marco è _____ come Silvia.

Activity C

Circle the correct answer.

1   Chi è la madre di mia sorella?

   a mia zia   **b mia madre**

2   Chi è il figlio di mio zio?

   a mio fratello   **b mio cugino**

3   Chi è il padre di mio padre?

   a mio nipote   **b mio nonno**

4   Chi è la figlia di mio padre?

   a mia cugina   **b mia sorella**

Activity D

Answer the following questions about your vacation.

1   Si è divertito/divertita?

_____

2   Dov'è andato/andata?

_____

3   Quando è arrivato/arrivata?

_____

4   Quanto tempo è rimasto/rimasta?

_____

5   Quando è rientrato/rientrata?

_____

Challenge

Can you think of 10 verbs that use *essere* in the *passato prossimo*?

Internet Activity

Want to send some online cards or postcards in Italian? Go to **www.berlitzbooks.com/5Mtravel** for a list of websites where you can send your friends and family *cartoline virtuali*.

A

a destra	ah <u>deh</u>-strah	on the right
a piedi	ah <u>pyeh</u>-dee	by foot
a presto!	ah <u>preh</u>-stoh	see you soon!
a sinistra	ah see-<u>nee</u>-strah	on the left
a tempo parziale	ah <u>tehm</u>-poh pahr-<u>tsyah</u>-leh	part time
a tempo pieno	ah <u>tehm</u>-poh <u>pyeh</u>-noh	full time
l'abbigliamento	lahb-bee-llyah-<u>mehn</u>-toh	clothing m
accanto a	ahk-<u>kahn</u>-toh ah	next to
accendere	ah-<u>chehn</u>-deh-reh	v to turn on
accessibile	ah-chehs-<u>see</u>-bee-leh	accessible m/f
l'accesso	lah-<u>chehs</u>-soh	n access
accettare	ah-cheht-<u>tah</u>-reh	v to accept
l'aceto	lah-<u>cheh</u>-toh	vinegar
l'acqua	<u>lahk</u>-kwah	n water f
l'acqua gassata	<u>lahk</u>-kwah gahs-<u>sah</u>-tah	sparkling water f
l'acqua naturale	<u>lahk</u>-kwah nah-too-<u>rah</u>-leh	still water f
l'adattatore	lah-daht-tah-<u>toh</u>-reh	adapter m
addormentarsi	ahd-dohr-mehn-<u>tahr</u>-see	v to fall asleep
l'aereo	lah-<u>eh</u>-reh-oh	airplane m
l'aeroporto	lah-eh-roh-<u>pohr</u>-toh	airport m
l'agenzia di viaggi	lah-gehn-<u>tsee</u>-ah dee <u>vyah</u>-djee	travel agency f
l'agnello	lah <u>nyehl</u>-loh	lamb m
aiutare	ah-yuu-<u>tah</u>-reh	v to help
aiuto!	ah-<u>yoo</u>-toh	help!
al fuoco!	ahl <u>fwoh</u>-koh	fire!
al ladro	ahl <u>lah</u>-droh	thief!
l'albergo	lahl-<u>behr</u>-goh	hotel m
l'alimentari	lah-lee-mehn-<u>tah</u>-ree	grocery store m sing.
allergico/allergica	ahl-<u>lehr</u>-jee-koh/ahl-<u>lehr</u>-jee-kah	allergic m/f
al sangue	ahl <u>sahn</u>-gweh	rare
alto/alta	<u>ahl</u>-toh/<u>ahl</u>-tah	tall m/f
altro/altra	<u>ahl</u>-troh/<u>ahl</u>-trah	other m/f
alzarsi	ahl-<u>tsahr</u>-see	v to get up
amare	ah-<u>mah</u>-reh	v to love
americano/ americana	ah-meh-ree-<u>kah</u>-noh/ ah-meh-ree-<u>kah</u>-nah	american m/f
gli amici	llyee ah-<u>mee</u>-chee	friends
anche	<u>ahn</u>-keh	also, as well, too
andare	ahn-<u>dah</u>-reh	v to go
andare a trovare	ahn-<u>dah</u>-reh ah troh-<u>vah</u>-reh	v to visit
l'anno	<u>lahn</u>-noh	year m
annullare	ahn-nool-<u>lah</u>-reh	v to cancel
l'antiacido	lahn-tee-<u>ah</u>-chee-doh	antiacid m
l'antiquariato	lahn-tee-kwah-<u>ryah</u>-toh	antique m
l'antipasto	lahn-tee-<u>pah</u>-stoh	appetizer m
l'antipasto misto	lahn-tee-<u>pah</u>-stoh <u>mee</u>-stoh	appetizer plate m
anziano/anziana	ahn-<u>tsyah</u>-noh/ahn-<u>tsyah</u>-nah	old (for people) m/f
l'aperitivo	lah-peh-ree-<u>tee</u>-voh	cocktail/before dinner drink m
aprire	ah-<u>pree</u>-reh	v to open
arancione	ah-rahn-<u>choh</u>-neh	orange
l'aria condizionata	<u>lah</u>-ryah kohn-dee-tsyoh-<u>nah</u>-tah	air conditioning f
arrivare	ahr-<u>ree</u>-vah-reh	v to arrive
gli arrivi	llyee ahr-<u>ree</u>-vee	arrivals
l'arte	<u>lahr</u>-teh	art f
l'ascensore	lah-shehn-<u>soh</u>-reh	elevator [lift] m
l'asciugamano	lah-shoo-gah-<u>mah</u>-noh	towel m
ascoltare	ah-skohl-<u>tah</u>-reh	v to listen to
asmatico/ asmatica	ah-<u>smah</u>-tee-koh/ ah-<u>smah</u>-tee-kah	asthmatic m/f
aspettare	ah-speht-<u>tah</u>-reh	v to wait (for)
l'aspirina	lah-spee-<u>ree</u>-nah	aspirin f
attenzione!	aht-tehn-<u>tsyoh</u>-neh	watch out!
attraversare	aht-trah-vehr-<u>sah</u>-reh	v to cross
l'Australia	low-<u>strah</u>-lyah	Australia f
australiano/ australiana	ow-strah-<u>lyah</u>-noh/ ow-strah-<u>lyah</u>-nah	Australian m/f
l'autista	low-<u>tee</u>-stah	driver m
l'auto	<u>low</u>-toh	car f
l'autobus	<u>low</u>-toh-boos	bus m
l'autobus notturno	<u>low</u>-toh-boos noht-<u>toor</u>-noh	night bus m
avere	ah-<u>veh</u>-reh	v to have
avere caldo	ah-<u>veh</u>-reh <u>kahl</u>-doh	v to be hot
avere fame	ah-<u>veh</u>-reh <u>fah</u>-meh	v to be hungry
avere freddo	ah-<u>veh</u>-reh <u>frehd</u>-doh	v to be cold
avere paura	ah-<u>veh</u>-reh pah-<u>oo</u>-rah	v to be afraid
avere sonno	ah-<u>veh</u>-reh <u>sohn</u>-noh	v to be sleepy

B

i baci	ee <u>bah</u>-chee	kisses
il bagaglio	eel bah-<u>gah</u>-llyoh	luggage
il bagaglio a mano	eel bah-<u>gah</u>-llyoh ah-<u>mah</u>-noh	carry-on bag
il bagno	eel <u>bah</u>-nyoh	bathroom
ballare	bahl-<u>lah</u>-reh	v to dance
la banca	lah <u>bahn</u>-kah	bank
il bancomat	eel <u>bahn</u>-koh-maht	ATM
la banconota	lah bahn-koh-<u>noh</u>-tah	bill
la bandiera	lah bahn-<u>dyeh</u>-rah	flag
il bar	eel <u>bahr</u>	bar
il barman/la barman	eel <u>bahr</u>-mahn/lah <u>bahr</u>-mahn	bartender m/f
basso/bassa	<u>bahs</u>-soh/<u>bahs</u>-sah	short m/f
belga	<u>behl</u>-gah	Belgian m/f
il Belgio	eel <u>behl</u>-jyoh	Belgium
bello/bella	<u>behl</u>-loh/<u>behl</u>-lah	beautiful m/f
bene	<u>beh</u>-neh	well adv
ben cotta	behn <u>koht</u>-tah	well done (steak)
benvenuti/ benvenute	behn-veh-<u>noo</u>-tee/ behn-veh-<u>noo</u>-teh	welcome m/f pl.
benvenuto/ benvenuta	behn-veh-<u>noo</u>-toh/ behn-veh-<u>noo</u>-tah	welcome m/f sing.
bere	<u>beh</u>-reh	v to drink
le bevande	leh beh-<u>vahn</u>-deh	drinks
bianco/bianca	<u>byahn</u>-koh/<u>byahn</u>-kah	white m/f
il bicchiere	eel beek-<u>kyeh</u>-reh	glass
la bicicletta	lah bee-chee-<u>kleht</u>-tah	bicyc
il biglietto	eel bee-<u>llyeht</u>-toh	ticket/bill
il bingo	eel <u>been</u>-goh	bingo
la birra	lah <u>beer</u>-rah	beer
la bistecca	lah bee-<u>stehk</u>-kah	steak
blu	bloo	blue
il bollitore	eel bohl-lee-<u>toh</u>-reh	electric kettle
la borsa	lah <u>bohr</u>-sah	bag
il borsellino	eel bohr-sehl-<u>lee</u>-noh	purse
la bottiglia	lah boht-<u>tee</u>-llyah	bottle
la bottiglia di vino	lah boht-<u>tee</u>-llyah dee <u>vee</u>-noh	bottle of wine
la bottiglia d'acqua	lah boht-<u>tee</u>-llyah <u>dahk</u>-kwah	bottle of water
la boutique	lah boo-<u>teek</u>	boutique

adj	adjective	v	verb	adv adverb	n noun

Italian	Pronunciation	English
il braccio/le braccia	eel brah-choh/leh brah-chah	arm/arms
brutto/brutta	broot-toh/broot-tah	ugly m/f
buon appetito	bwoh ahp-peh-tee-toh	enjoy your meal
buongiorno	bwohn-jyohr-noh	good morning
buon	bwohn	good m sing.
buono/buona	bwoh-noh/bwoh-nah	good m/f
buonasera	bwoh-nah seh-rah	good evening
buoni/buone	bwoh-nee/bwoh-neh	good m/f pl
il/la buttafuori	eel/lah boot-tah-fwoh-ree	bouncer m/f

C

cadere	kah-deh-reh	v to fall
il caffè	eel kahf-feh	coffee
il caffè macchiato	eel kahf-feh mahk-kyah-toh	coffe with a little milk
cambiare	kahm-byah-reh	v to change/to exchange
il cambio	eel kahm-byoh	n change
la camera	lah kah-meh-rah	room
la camera doppia	lah kah-meh-rah dohp-pyah	double room
la camicia	lah kah-mee-chah	shirt
camminare	kahm-mee-nah-reh	v to walk
i capelli	ee kah-pehl-lee	hair
capire	kah-pee-reh	v to understand
il capolinea	eel kah-poh-lee-neh-ah	last stop
il cappellino	eel kahp-pehl-lee-noh	hat
il cappotto	eel kahp-poht-toh	coat
il cappuccino	eel kahp-poo-chee-noh	cappuccino
il carabiniere	eel kah-rah-bee-neeyeh-reh	police officer
i carciofi	ee kahr-choh-fee	artichokes
carino/carina	kah-ree-noh/kah-ree-nah	pretty m/f
la carne	lah kahr-neh	meat
caro/cara	kah-roh/kah-rah	expensive/dear m/f
il carrello	eel kahr-rehl-loh	baggage cart
la carta d'imbarco	lah kahr-tah deem-bahr-koh	boarding pass
la carta di credito	lah kahr-tah dee kreh-dee-toh	credit card
la carta igienica	lah kahr-tah ee-jyeh-nee-kah	toilet paper
la carta telefonica	lah kahr-tah teh-leh-foh-nee-kah	telephone card
la cartina	lah kahr-tee-nah	map
la cartolina	lah kahr-toh-lee-nah	postcard
la casa	lah kah-sah	home/house
il casinò	eel kah-zee-noh	casino
la cassa	lah kahs-sah	cash registrer
il cassiere	eel kahs-syeh-reh	cashier
il castello	eel kah-stehl-loh	castle
cattivo/cattiva	kaht-tee-voh/kaht-tee-vah	bad m/f
c'è	cheh	there is
il cellulare	eel chehl-loo-lah-reh	cell phone
la cena	lah cheh-nah	dinner
il centesimo	eel chehn-teh-zee-moh	cent
il centro commerciale	eel chehn-troh kohm-mehr-chah-leh	shopping mall
cercare	chehr-kah-reh	v to look for
i cerotti	ee cheh-roht-tee	bandages
certo	chehr-toh	certain
che (cosa)	keh (koh-zah)	what
il check-in	eel chehk-een	n check-in
chi	kee	who
chiamare	kyah-mah-reh	v to call
chiamarsi	kyah-mahr-see	v to call oneself/to be named
la chiave	lah kyah-veh	key
la chiavetta USB	lah kyah-veht-tah oo-ehs-bee	USB key
chiedere	kyeh-deh-reh	v to ask
la chiesa	lah kyeh-zah	church
chiudere	kyuh-deh-reh	v to close
ci sono	chee soh-noh	there are
il cibo	eel chee-boh	food
il cinema	eel chee-neh-mah	movie theater
la cintura	lah cheen-too-rah	belt
la cioccolata calda	lah chohk-koh-lah-tah kahl-dah	hot chocolate
la città	lah cheet-tah	city/town
la cittadinanza	lah cheet-tah-dee-nahn-tsah	citizenship
cliccare	kleek-kah-reh	v to click
la cola	lah koh-lah	cola
la cola light	lah koh-lah lah-eet	diet cola
il cognome	eel koh-nyoh-meh	surname
la colazione	lah koh-lah-tsyoh-neh	breakfast
il colore degli occhi	eel koh-loh-reh deh-lly ohk-kee	eye color
il coltello	eel kohl-tehl-loh	knife
come	koh-meh	how
il commissariato	eel kohm-mees-sah-ryah-toh	police station
comodo/comoda	koh-moh-doh/koh-moh-dah	comfortable m/f
il compagno/ la compagna	eel kohm-pah-nyoh/ lah kohm-pah-nyah	partner m/f
comprare	kohm-prah-reh	v to buy
il computer	eel kohm-pyoo-tehr	computer
con	kohn	with
il concerto	eel kohn-chehr-toh	concert
confermare	kohn-fehr-mah-reh	v to confirm
la connessione internet	lah kohn-nehs-syoh-neh een-tehr-neht	internet access
connettersi	kohn-neht-tehr-see	v to connect
conoscere	koh-noh-sheh-reh	v to meet/to know
consigliare	kohn-see-llyah-reh	v to recommend/to advise
la consumazione	lah kohn-soo-mah-tsyoh-neh	n drink
i contanti	ee kohn-tahn-tee	cash
continuare	kohn-tee-noo-ah-reh	v to continue
il conto	eel kohn-toh	the check
i contorni	ee kohn-tohr-nee	side dishes
controllare	kohn-trohl-lah-reh	v to check
il controllo passaporti	eel kohn-trohl-loh pahs-sah-pohr-tee	passport control
la coperta	lah koh-pehr-tah	blanket
il coperto	eel koh-pehr-toh	cover change
la cornetta	lah kohr-neht-tah	receiver
la cortesia	lah kohr-teh-zee-ah	kindness
cosa?	koh-sah	what?
la cosa	lah koh-zah	thing
i cosmetici	ee koh-smeh-tee-chee	beauty products
costare	koh-stah-reh	v to cost
le cozze	leh koh-tseh	mussels
la cravatta	lah krah-vaht-tah	tie
il credito	eel kreh-dee-toh	units remaining on the card
la crociera	lah kroh-cheh-rah	cruise
il cucchiaio	eel kook-kyah-yoh	spoon
la cucina	lah koo-chee-nah	cooking
il cugino/la cugina	eel koo-jee-noh/lah koo-jee-nah	cousin m/f
il cuscino	eel koo-shee-noh	pillow

adj   adjective   v   verb   adv   adverb   n   noun

D

dare	<u>dah</u>-reh	v to give
dare un'occhiata	<u>dah</u>-reh oon-ohk-<u>kyah</u>-tah	v to browse
la data	lah <u>dah</u>-tah	date
la data di nascita	lah <u>dah</u>-tah dee <u>nah</u>-shee-tah	date of birth
davanti a	dah-<u>vahn</u>-tee ah	in front of
il dazio doganale	eel <u>dah</u>-tsyoh doh-gah-<u>nah</u>-leh	customs duty
il decimo/	eel <u>deh</u>-chee-moh/	tenth m/f
la decima	lah <u>deh</u>-chee-mah	
il dente/i denti	eel <u>dehn</u>-teh/ee <u>dehn</u>-tee	tooth/teeth
il deposito bagagli	eel deh-<u>poh</u>-zee-toh bah-<u>gah</u>-llyee	luggage storage
il dessert	eel dehs-<u>sehrt</u>	dessert
la destinazione	lah deh-stee-nah-<u>tsyoh</u>-neh	destination
di fronte a	dee <u>frohn</u>-teh ah	across from
di niente	dee <u>neeyehn</u>-teh	don't mention it
diabetico/	dyah-<u>beh</u>-tee-koh/	diabetic m/f
diabetica	dyah-<u>beh</u>-tee-kah	
dichiarare	dee-kyah-<u>rah</u>-reh	v to declare
la dichiarazione	lah dee-kyah-rah-<u>tsyoh</u>-neh	customs declaration
doganale	doh-gah-<u>nah</u>-leh	
dietro a	<u>dyeh</u>-troh ah	behind
il digestivo	eel dee-jeh-<u>stee</u>-voh	liqueur/after dinner drink
digitare	dee-jee-<u>tah</u>-reh	v to dial
i dipinti	ee dee-<u>peen</u>-tee	paintings
dire	<u>dee</u>-reh	v to say/to tell
la direzione	lah dee-reh-<u>tsyoh</u>-neh	direction
il disastro	eel dee-<u>sah</u>-stroh	disaster
la discoteca	lah dee-skoh-<u>teh</u>-kah	club
il disegno	eel dee-<u>seh</u>-nyoh	drawing
il dito/le dita	eel <u>dee</u>-toh/leh <u>dee</u>-tah	finger/fingers
divertente	dee-vehr-<u>tehn</u>-teh	fun
divertirsi	dee-vehr-<u>teer</u>-see	v to enjoy oneself
il DJ	eel dee-<u>jay</u>	dj
la doccia	lah <u>doh</u>-chah	shower
il documento	eel doh-koo-<u>mehn</u>-toh	document
la dogana	lah doh-<u>gah</u>-nah	custom
il dolce	eel <u>dohl</u>-cheh	cake/dessert
i dollari	ee <u>dohl</u>-lah-ree	dollars
la domanda	lah doh-<u>mahn</u>-dah	question
domandare	doh-mahn-<u>dah</u>-reh	v to ask
domani	doh-<u>mah</u>-nee	tomorrow adv
la donna	lah <u>dohn</u>-nah	woman
dopo	<u>doh</u>-poh	after
dormire	dohr-<u>mee</u>-reh	v to sleep
dove	<u>doh</u>-veh	where
dov'è	dohv <u>eh</u>	where is
dovere	doh-<u>veh</u>-reh	v must
il drink	eel dreenk	n drink

E

gli effetti personali	llyee ehf-<u>feht</u>-tee pehr-soh-<u>nah</u>-lee	personal belongings
eliminare	eh-lee-mee-<u>nah</u>-reh	v to delete
l'e-mail	leeh-<u>mayl</u>	n e-mail f
l'enoteca	leh-noh-<u>teh</u>-kah	wine store f
entrare	ehn-<u>trah</u>-reh	v to enter
l'entrata libera	lehn-<u>trah</u>-tah <u>lee</u>-beh-rah	free admission f

l'escursione	leh-skoor-<u>syoh</u>-neh	hike f
essere	ehs-<u>seh</u>-reh	v to be
essere in pensione	ehs-<u>seh</u>-reh een pehn-<u>syoh</u>-neh	v to be retired
essere lontano	ehs-<u>seh</u>-reh lohn-<u>tah</u>-noh	v to be far from
l'est	lehst	east m
l'euro	leh-oo-roh	euro m

F

fa bel tempo	fah behl <u>tehm</u>-poh	it's nice out
fa brutto tempo	fah <u>broot</u>-toh <u>tehm</u>-poh	the weather is bad
fa caldo	fah <u>kahl</u>-doh	it's hot
fa freddo	fah <u>frehd</u>-doh	it's cold
la famiglia	lah fah-<u>mee</u>-llyah	family
fantastico/	fahn-<u>tah</u>-stee-koh/	fantastic [brilliant] m/f
fantastica	fahn-<u>tah</u>-stee-kah	
fare	<u>fah</u>-reh	v to do
fare attenzione	<u>fah</u>-reh aht-tehn-<u>tsyoh</u>-neh	v to pay attention
fare il biglietto	<u>fah</u>-reh eel bee-<u>llyeht</u>-toh	v to buy a ticket
fare la fila	<u>fah</u>-reh lah <u>fee</u>-lah	v to stand in line
fare in fretta	<u>fah</u>-reh een <u>freht</u>-tah	v to hurry
fare shopping	<u>fah</u>-re <u>shohp</u>-peeng	v to go shopping
fare spese	<u>fah</u>-reh <u>speh</u>-zeh	v to go shopping
fare sport	<u>fah</u>-reh spohrt	v to practice sports
fare surf	<u>fah</u>-reh sehrf	v to surf
fare un'escursione	<u>fah</u>-reh oon eh-skoor-<u>syoh</u>-neh	v to hike
fare una passeggiata	<u>fah</u>-reh oo-nah pahs-seh-<u>djyah</u>-tah	v to take a walk
fare le valigie	<u>fah</u>-reh leh vah-<u>lee</u>-jyeh	v to pack one's bags
la farmacia	lah fahr-mah-<u>chee</u>-ah	pharmacy
la farmacia	lah fahr-mah-<u>chee</u>-ah	all-night pharmacy
notturna	noht-<u>toor</u>-nah	
farsi la barba	<u>fahr</u>-see lah <u>bahr</u>-bah	v to shave
farsi la doccia	<u>fahr</u>-see lah <u>doh</u>-chah	v to take a shower
la fattura	lah faht-<u>too</u>-rah	invoice
la febbre	lah <u>fehb</u>-breh	fever
la fermata	lah fehr-<u>mah</u>-tah	stop
la fermata	lah fehr-<u>mah</u>-tah	bus stop
dell'autobus	dehl-<u>low</u>-toh-boos	
il ferro da stiro	eel <u>fehr</u>-roh dah <u>stee</u>-roh	n iron
la festa	lah <u>feh</u>-stah	party
le fettuccine	leh feht-too-<u>chee</u>-neh	egg pasta
i figli	ee <u>fee</u>-llyee	children
la figlia	lah <u>fee</u>-llyah	daughter
il figlio	eel <u>fee</u>-llyoh	son
il file	eel <u>fah</u>-eel	n file
il film	eel feelm	film
il filtro solare	eel <u>feel</u>-troh soh-<u>lah</u>-reh	sunscreen
finire	fee-<u>nee</u>-reh	v to finish/to end
il fioraio	eel fyoh-<u>rah</u>-yoh	flower shop
il fiume	eel <u>fyoo</u>-meh	river
il fon	eel fohn	hairdryer
la fontana	lah fohn-<u>tah</u>-nah	fountain
la forchetta	lah fohr-<u>keht</u>-tah	fork
il formaggio	eel fohr-<u>mah</u>-djyoh	cheese
il forno a legna	eel <u>fohr</u>-noh ah <u>leh</u>-nyah	wood-burning oven
la foto	lah <u>foh</u>-toh	picture
francese	frahn-<u>cheh</u>-seh	adj French m/f
il francese	eel frahn-<u>cheh</u>-seh	n French
la Francia	lah <u>frahn</u>-cha	France

adj adjective	v verb	adv adverb	n noun

Italian	Pronunciation	English
il fratello	eel frah-<u>tehl</u>-loh	brother
la frutta	lah <u>froot</u>-tah	fruit
fumatore	foo-mah-<u>toh</u>-reh	smoker
funzionare	foon-tsyoh-<u>nah</u>-reh	v to work (object)

G

la gamba/le gambe	lah <u>gahm</u>-bah/leh <u>gahm</u>-beh	leg/legs
i gamberetti	ee gahm-beh-<u>reht</u>-tee	shrimp
il gelato	eel jeh-<u>lah</u>-toh	ice cream
i genitori	ee jeh-nee-<u>toh</u>-ree	parents
gentile	jehn-<u>tee</u>-leh	nice
la Germania	lah jehr-<u>mah</u>-neeyah	Germany
la giacca	lah <u>jyahk</u>-kah	jacket
giallo/gialla	<u>jyahl</u>-loh/<u>jyahl</u>-lah	yellow m/f
il ginocchio/	eel jee-<u>nohk</u>-kyoh/	knee/knees
le ginocchia	leh jee-<u>nohk</u>-kyah	
il giocattolo	eel jyoh-<u>kaht</u>-toh-loh	toy
la gioielleria	lah jyoh-yehl-leh-<u>ree</u>-ah	jewelry store
il gioiello	eel jyoh-<u>yehl</u>-loh	piece of jewelry
i giorni	ee <u>jyohr</u>-nee	days
il giorno	eel <u>jyohr</u>-noh	day
giovane	<u>jyoh</u>-vah-neh	young m/f
girare	jee-<u>rah</u>-reh	v to turn
il giubbino	eel joob-<u>bee</u>-noh	sport jacket
gli gnocchi	llyee <u>nyohk</u>-kee	small potato dumplings
la gola	lah <u>goh</u>-lah	throat
grande	<u>grahn</u>-deh	big m/f
il grande magazzino	eel <u>grahn</u>-deh mah-gah-<u>tsee</u>-noh	department store
grandi	<u>grahn</u>-dee	big m/f pl.
gratuito	grah-<u>too</u>-ee-toh	free
grazie	<u>grah</u>-tsyeh	thank you
grigio/grigia	<u>gree</u>-jyoh/<u>gree</u>-jyah	grey m/f
guardare	gwahr-<u>dah</u>-reh	v to look at
il guardaroba	eel gwahr-dah-<u>roh</u>-bah	coat check
la guida	lah <u>gwee</u>-dah	guide book

H

l'hotspot	<u>lhoht</u>-spoht	hotspot m

I

ieri	<u>yeh</u>-ree	yesterday adv
il/la farmacista	eel/lah fahr-mah-<u>chee</u>-stah	pharmacist m/f
imparare	eem-pah-<u>rah</u>-reh	v to learn
l'importo da pagare	leem-<u>pohr</u>-toh dah pah-<u>gah</u>-reh	total due m
in contatto	een kohn-<u>taht</u>-toh	in touch
in fondo a	een <u>fohn</u>-doh ah	at the end of
in ritardo	een ree-<u>tahr</u>-doh	late
incartare	een-kahr-<u>tah</u>-reh	v to wrap
incredibile	een-kreh-<u>dee</u>-bee-leh	incredible m/f
indicare	een-dee-<u>kah</u>-reh	v to show
le indicazioni	leh een-dee-kah-<u>tsyoh</u>-nee	directions f pl.
l'indigestione	leen-dee-jeh-<u>styoh</u>-neh	indigestion m
l'indirizzo	leen-dee-<u>ree</u>-tsoh	address m
l'infermiere/	leen-fehr-<u>myeh</u>-reh/	nurse m/f
l'infermiera	leen-fehr-<u>myeh</u>-rah	
l'influenza	leen-floo-<u>ehn</u>-tsah	flu f

Italian	Pronunciation	English
le informazioni	leh een-fohr-mah-<u>tsyoh</u>-nee	information f pl.
l'Inghilterra	leen-gheel-<u>tehr</u>-rah	England f
inglese	een-<u>gleh</u>-zeh	adj English m/f
l'inglese	leen-<u>gleh</u>-zeh	n English m
l'ingresso	leen-<u>grehs</u>-soh	cover charge
iniziare	ee-nee-<u>tsyah</u>-reh	v to begin
l'insalata	leen-sah-<u>lah</u>-tah	salad f
l'insalata di	leen-sah-<u>lah</u>-tah dee	seafood salad
frutti di mare	<u>froot</u>-tee dee <u>mah</u>-reh	
insieme	een-<u>syeh</u>-meh	together adv
interessante	een-teh-rehs-<u>sahn</u>-teh	interesting
internazionale	een-tehr-nah-tsyoh-<u>nah</u>-leh	international
internet	een-tehr-neht	internet
l'internet point	leen-tehr-neht <u>poh</u>-eent	internet point m
introdurre	een-troh-<u>door</u>-reh	v to insert
inviare	een-vee-<u>ah</u>-reh	v to send
l'Italia	lee-<u>tah</u>-lyah	Italy f
italiano/italiana	ee-tah-<u>lyah</u>-noh/ee-tah-<u>lyah</u>-nah	adj Italian m/f
l'italiano	lee-tah-<u>lyah</u>-noh	n Italian m
l'IVA	<u>lee</u>-vah	value-added tax

J

il jazz	eel jahz	jazz
il jazz club	eel jahz-<u>cloob</u>	jazz club
i jeans	ee <u>jee</u>-ns	jeans

L

la lampada	lah <u>lahm</u>-pah-dah	lamp
le lasagne	leh lah-<u>zah</u>-nyeh	lasagna
lasciare	lah-<u>shah</u>-reh	v to leave
il latte	eel <u>laht</u>-teh	n milk
il lavandino	eel lah-vahn-<u>dee</u>-noh	sink
lavarsi	lah-<u>vahr</u>-see	v to wash oneself
lavorare	lah-voh-<u>rah</u>-reh	v to work
leggere	<u>leh</u>-djeh-reh	v to read
lentamente	lehn-tah-<u>mehn</u>-teh	slowly adv
le lenzuola	leh lehn-<u>tswoh</u>-lah	sheets f pl.
il lenzuolo	eel lehn-<u>tswoh</u>-loh	sheet
il lettino	eel leht-<u>tee</u>-noh	crib
il letto	eel <u>leht</u>-toh	bed
il letto matrimoniale	eel <u>leht</u>-toh mah-tree-moh-<u>neeyah</u>-leh	double bed
il letto singolo	eel <u>leht</u>-toh <u>seen</u>-goh-loh	single bed
il letto supplementare	eel <u>leht</u>-toh soop-pleh-mehn-<u>tah</u>-reh	extra bed
lì	lee	there adv
lì vicino	lee vee-<u>cee</u>-noh	close to there
la libreria	lah lee-breh-<u>ree</u>-ah	bookstore
il libro	eel <u>lee</u>-broh	book
la linea	lah <u>lee</u>-nehah	line
la lingua	lah <u>leen</u>-gwah	language/tongue
il link	eel leenk	n link
lontano da	lohn-<u>tah</u>-noh dah	far from
lungo	<u>loon</u>-goh	long
il luogo di nascita	eel <u>lwoh</u>-goh dee <u>nah</u>-shee-tah	place of birth

adj	adjective	v	verb	adv	adverb	n	noun

Italian–English Glossary

M

ma	mah	but adv
la macchina	lah mahk-kee-nah	machine
la madre	lah mah-dreh	mother
il maglione	eel mah-llyoh-neh	sweater
magnifico/ magnifica	mah-nyee-fee-koh/ mah-nyee-fee-kah	magnificent m/f
mai	mah-ee	never adv
il maiale	eel mah-yah-leh	pork
il mal d'auto	eel mahl dow-toh	carsick
il mal di gola	eel mahl dee goh-lah	sore throat
il mal di stomaco	eel mahl dee stoh-mah-koh	stomach pains
il mal di testa	eel mahl dee teh-stah	headache
malato/malata	mah-lah-toh/mah-lah-tah	sick m/f
mancare	mahn-kah-reh	v to miss
la mancia	lah mahn-cha	tip
mandare	mahn-dah-reh	v to send
mangiare	mahn-jyah-reh	v to eat
la mano/le mani	lah mah-noh/leh mah nee	hand/hands
il manzo	eel mahn-dzoh	beef
la mappa	lah mahp-pah	map
il marito	eel mah-ree-toh	husband
marrone	mahr-roh-neh	brown
la mattina	lah maht-tee-nah	morning
media	meh-dyah	medium (steak)
il medico	eel meh-dee-koh	doctor
meglio	meh-llyoh	better adv
le melanzane	leh meh-lahn-dzah-neh	eggplants
il melone	eel meh-loh-neh	melon
il menù	eel meh-noo	menu
il menù del giorno	eel meh-noo dehl jyohr-noh	prix-fixed menu
il mercato	eel mehr-kah-toh	market
il merluzzo	eel mehr-loo-tsoh	cod
il mese	eel meh-zeh	month
il messaggio di posta elettronica	eel mehs-sah-djyoh dee poh-stah eh-leht-troh-nee-kah	e-mail
la metro	lah meh-troh	subway
mezzanotte	meh-dzdah-noht-teh	midnight
mezzo	meh-dzoh	half
mezzogiorno	meh-dzoh-jyohr-noh	noon
mi chiamo	mee kyah-moh	my name is
mi dispiace	mee dee-spyah-cheh	I'm sorry
mi piace	mee pyah-cheh	I like
mi scusi	mee skoo-zee	excuse me
il migliore/ la migliore	eel mee-llyoh-reh/ lah mee-llyoh-reh	the best m/f
la minestra	lah mee-neh-strah	soup
la miniatura	lah mee-neeyah-too-rah	miniature
la moda	lah moh-dah	fashion
modificare	moh-dee-fee-kah-reh	v to modify
la moglie	lah moh-llyeh	wife
molto	mohl-toh	much
molto/molta	mohl-toh/mohl-tah	a lot of m/f
la moneta	lah moh-neh-tah	coin
il monumento	eel moh-noo-mehn-toh	monument
morire	moh-ree-reh	v to die
il motivo	eel moh-tee-voh	purpose
il mouse	eel mows	mouse

il museo	eel moo-zeh-oh	museum
la musica classica	lah moo-zee-kah klahs-see-kah	classical music
la musica pop	lah moo-zee-kah pohp	pop music

N

nascere	nah-sheh-reh	v to be born
il naso	eel nah-soh	nose
la nausea	lah now-zeh-ah	nausea
la navetta	lah nah-veht-tah	shuttle
la nazionalità	lah nah-tsyoh-nah-lee-tah	nationality
il negozio	eel neh-goh-tsyoh	store (shop)
il negozio di regali	eel neh-goh-tsyoh dee reh-gah-lee	gift shop
nero/nera	neh-roh/neh-rah	black m/f
nessuno	nehs-soo-noh	nobody
nessun(o)/nessuna	nehs-soo-n(oh)/nehs-soo-nah	adj no m/f
niente	neeyehn-teh	nothing
il/la nipote	eel/lah nee-poh-teh	grandson/nephew; grandaughter/niece
no	noh	no adv
noioso/noiosa	noh-yoh-soh/noh-yoh-sah	boring m/f
noleggiare	noh-leh-djyah-reh	v to rent
il nome	eel noh-meh	first name
non	nohn	not adv
non disturbare	nohn dee-stoor-bah-reh	v do not disturb
la nonna	lah nohn-nah	grandmother
il nonno	eel nohn-noh	grandfather
il nono/la nona	eel noh-noh/lah noh-nah	ninth m/f
il nord	eel nohrd	north
la notte	lah noht-teh	night
il numero	eel noo-meh-roh	number
il numero del volo	eel noo-meh-roh dehl voh-loh	flight number
il numero di telefono	eel noo-meh-roh dee teh-leh-foh-noh	phone number
il numero verde	eel noo-meh-roh vehr-deh	toll-free number
nuovo/nuova	nwoh-voh/nwoh-vah	new m/f

O

l'occhio/gli occhi	lok-kyoh/llyee ok-kee	eye/eyes
offrire	ohf-free-reh	v to offer
oggi	oh-djee	today adv
l'olio	loh-lyoh	oil
online	ohn-lah-een	online
l'opera	loh-peh-rah	opera f
l'orario dei voli	loh-rah-ryoh day voh-lee	flight status
l'orecchio/le orecchie	loh-rehk-kyoh/leh oh-rehk-kyeh	ear/ears
orribile	ohr-ree-bee-leh	horrible m/f
l'ospedale	loh-speh-dah-leh	hospital m
l'ospitalità	loh-spee-tah-lee-tah	hospitality f
l'ottavo/l'ottava	loht-tah-voh/loht-tah-vah	eighth m/f
l'ovest	loh-vehst	west m

P

il pacchetto di biglietti	eel pahk-keht-toh dee bee-llyeht-tee	booklet of tickets
il pacchetto regalo	eel pahk-keht-toh reh-gah-loh	gift wrap
il padre	eel pah-dreh	father

---

adj adjective	v verb	adv adverb	n noun

il paese	eel pah-<u>eh</u>-zeh	country, village
pagare	pah-<u>gah</u>-reh	v to pay
il palazzo comunale	eel pah-<u>lah</u>-tsoh koh-moo-<u>nah</u>-leh	town hall
il pane	eel <u>pah</u>-neh	bread
la panetteria	lah pah-neht-teh-<u>ree</u>-ah	bakery
i pantaloni	ee pahn-tah-<u>loh</u>-nee	pants
il parcheggio dei taxi	eel pahr-<u>keh</u>-djyoh day <u>tah</u>-ksee	taxi stand
il parco	eel <u>pahr</u>-koh	n park
parlare	pahr-<u>lah</u>-reh	v to speak
la partenza	lah pahr-<u>tehn</u>-tsah	departure
partire	pahr-<u>tee</u>-reh	v to leave
il passaporto	eel pahs-sah-<u>pohr</u>-toh	passport
passare	pahs-<u>sah</u>-reh	v to pass
il passeggero	eel pahs-seh-<u>djeh</u>-roh	passenger
la password	lah <u>pahs</u>-wohrd	password
la pasticceria	lah pah-stee-cheh-<u>ree</u>-ah	pastry shop
le pasticche per la gola	leh pah-<u>steek</u>-keh pehr lah <u>goh</u>-lah	throat lozenges
le patate	leh pah-<u>tah</u>-teh	potatoes
il/la peggiore	eel/lah peh-<u>djyoh</u>-reh	the worst m/f
la pelletteria	lah pehl-leht-teh-<u>ree</u>-ah	leather goods store
pensare	pehn-<u>sah</u>-reh	v to think
i peperoni	ee peh-peh-<u>roh</u>-nee	peppers
per favore	pehr fah-<u>voh</u>-reh	please adv
perché	pehr-<u>keh</u>	why/because adv
perdere	<u>pehr</u>-deh-reh	v to lose
perfetto	pehr-<u>feht</u>-toh	perfect
Permesso?	pehr-<u>mehs</u>-soh	May I come through?
le persone	leh pehr-<u>soh</u>-neh	people
il pesce	eel <u>peh</u>-sheh	n fish
pessimo/pessima	<u>pehs</u>-see-moh/<u>pehs</u>-see-mah	awful m/f
il petto	eel <u>peht</u>-toh	chest
piacere	pyah-<u>cheh</u>-reh	v to be pleasing to
piacere!	pyah-<u>cheh</u>-reh	nice to meet you!
il piano	eel <u>pyah</u>-noh	floor
il piano terra	eel <u>pyah</u>-noh <u>tehr</u>-rah	ground floor
il piatto	eel <u>pyaht</u>-toh	plate
la piazza	lah <u>pyah</u>-tsah	town square
piccolo/piccola	<u>peek</u>-koh-loh/<u>peek</u>-koh-lah	small m/f
il piede/i piedi	eel <u>pyeh</u>-deh/ee <u>pyeh</u>-dee	foot/feet
la pista da ballo	lah <u>pee</u>-stah dah <u>bahl</u>-loh	dance floor
più	pyoo	more adv
la pizza	lah <u>pee</u>-tsah	pizza
la polizia	lah poh-lee-<u>tsee</u>-ah	police
il poliziotto	eel poh-lee-<u>tsyoht</u>-toh	police officer
il pollo	eel <u>pohl</u>-loh	chicken
il pomeriggio	eel poh-meh-<u>ree</u>-djoh	afternoon
il ponte	eel <u>pohn</u>-teh	bridge
il portachiavi	eel pohr-tah-<u>kyah</u>-vee	keychain
portare	pohr-<u>tah</u>-reh	v to bring
il portatile	eel pohr-<u>tah</u>-tee-leh	laptop
la posta elettronica	lah <u>poh</u>-stah eh-leht-<u>troh</u>-nee-kah	e-mail
il posto	eel <u>poh</u>-stoh	seat
potere	poh-<u>teh</u>-reh	v can/to be able
il pranzo	eel <u>prahn</u>-tsoh	lunch
preferire	preh-feh-<u>ree</u>-reh	v to prefer
prego	<u>preh</u>-goh	you are welcome
Prego?	<u>preh</u>-goh	Can I help you?
prendere	<u>prehn</u>-deh-reh	v to take
prenotare	preh-noh-<u>tah</u>-reh	v to reserve
la prenotazione	lah preh-noh-tah-<u>tsyoh</u>-neh	reservation
presto	<u>preh</u>-stoh	early
prima	<u>pree</u>-mah	before adv
i primi piatti	ee <u>pree</u>-mee <u>pyaht</u>-tee	first courses
il primo/la prima	eel <u>pree</u>-moh/lah <u>pree</u>-mah	first m/f
i prodotti locali	ee proh-<u>doht</u>-tee loh-<u>kah</u>-lee	local products
la profumeria	lah proh-foo-meh-<u>ree</u>-ah	perfume store
il profumo	eel proh-<u>foo</u>-moh	perfume/cologne
il pronto soccorso	eel <u>prohn</u>-toh sohk-<u>kohr</u>-soh	emergency room
pronto?	<u>prohn</u>-toh	hello?
il prosciutto	eel proh-<u>shoot</u>-toh	cured ham
il prossimo	eel <u>prohs</u>-see-moh	next
il pub	eel pahb	pub
pulito/pulita	poo-<u>lee</u>-toh/poo-<u>lee</u>-tah	clean m/f

Q

il quadro	eel <u>kwah</u>-droh	picture
qual è?	<u>kwah</u>-leh	what is?
qualcosa	<u>kwahl</u>-<u>koh</u>-zah	anything/something
quale	<u>kwah</u>-leh	what/which
quali	<u>kwah</u>-lee	what/which m/f pl.
quando	<u>kwahn</u>-doh	when adv
il quarto/la quarta	eel <u>kwahr</u>-toh/lah <u>kwahr</u>-tah	fourth m/f
un quarto	oon <u>kwahr</u>-toh	a quarter
quelli/quelle	<u>kwehl</u>-lee/<u>kwehl</u>-leh	those m/f pl.
quello/quella	<u>kwehl</u>-loh/<u>kwehl</u>-lah	that m/f sing.
questi/queste	<u>kweh</u>-stee/<u>kweh</u>-steh	these m/f pl.
questo/questa	<u>kweh</u>-stoh/<u>kweh</u>-stah	this m/f sing.
qui	kwee	here adv
qui di fronte	kwee dee <u>frohn</u>-teh	across the way
qui vicino	kwee vee-<u>chee</u>-noh	close to here
il quinto/la quinta	eel <u>kween</u>-toh/lah <u>kween</u>-tah	fifth m/f

R

il raffreddore	eel rahf-frehd-<u>doh</u>-reh	n cold
il rap	eel rahp	rap
il regalo	eel reh-<u>gah</u>-loh	present
la regione	lah reh-<u>jyoh</u>-neh	region
la residenza	lah reh-see-<u>dehn</u>-tsah	residence
il resto	eel <u>reh</u>-stoh	change
il resto massimo	ell <u>reh</u>-stoh <u>mahs</u>-see-moh	maximum change
riagganciare	ryah-gahn-<u>chah</u>-reh	v to hang up
ricaricare	ree-kah-ree-<u>kah</u>-reh	v to reload
la ricetta	lah ree-<u>cheht</u>-tah	prescription
la ricevuta	lah ree-ceh-<u>voo</u>-tah	receipt
richiamare	ree-kyah-<u>mah</u>-reh	v to call back
rientrare	ryehn-<u>trah</u>-reh	v to go home
rifare (la camera)	ree-<u>fah</u>-reh (lah <u>kah</u>-meh-rah)	v to clean (room)
rimanere	ree-mah-<u>neh</u>-reh	v to stay
rinnovare	reen-noh-<u>vah</u>-reh	v to renew
ripetere	ree-<u>peh</u>-teh-reh	v to repeat
riposarsi	ree-poh-<u>sahr</u>-see	v to rest
rispondere	ree-<u>spohn</u>-deh-reh	v to answer
il ristorante	eel ree-stoh-<u>rahn</u>-teh	restaurant

adj	adjective	v	verb	adv
adverb			n	noun

ritirare	ree-tee-rah-reh	v to collect/to remove
il ritiro bagagli	ell ree-tee-roh bah-gah-llyee	baggage claim
ritornare	ree-tohr-nah-reh	v to go back
riuscire	ryoo-shee-reh	v to succeed
rivedere	ree-veh-deh-reh	v to see again
il rock	eel rohk	rock music
romantico/ romantica	roh-mahn-tee-koh/ roh-mahn-tee-kah	romantic m/f
rompersi	rohm-pehr-see	v to break (one's arm/leg)
rosa	roh-zah	pink
rosso/rossa	rohs-soh/rohs-sah	red m/f

S

salire	sah-lee-reh	v to go up/to get on
il salmone	eel sahl-moh-neh	salmon
salvare	sahl-vah-reh	v to save
la saponetta	lah sah-poh-neht-tah	soap
sbagliare	sbah-llyah-reh	v to make a mistake
la scala	lah skah-lah	staircase
lo scalo	loh skah-loh	stopover
scaricare	skah-ree-kah-reh	v to download
le scarpe	leh skahr-peh	shoes
la scatola di cioccolatini	lah skah-toh-lah dee chohk-koh-lah-tee-nee	box of chocolates
scegliere	sheh-llyeh-reh	v to choose
scendere	shehn-deh-reh	v to go down/to get off
lo schermo	loh skehr-moh	screen
la schiena	lah skyeh-nah	back
sciare	shee-ah-reh	v to ski
la sciarpa	lah shahr-pah	scarf
scippare	sheep-pah-reh	v to rob
lo sciroppo per la tosse	loh shee-rohp-poh pehr-lah-tohs-seh	cough syrup
lo sconto	loh skohn-toh	discount
lo scontrino	loh skohn-tree-noh	receipt
la scrivania	lah skree-vah-nee-ah	desk
scrivere	skree-veh-reh	v to write/to type
le sculture	leh skool-tooh-reh	sculptures
il secondo	eel seh-kohn-doh	main course
il secondo/ la seconda	eel seh-kohn-doh/ lah seh-kohn-dah	second m/f
sedersi	seh-dehr-see	v to sit
selezionare	seh-leh-tsyoh-nah-reh	v to select
sempre	sehm-preh	always adv
sentire	sehn-tee-reh	v to hear/to feel
sentirsi bene	sehn-teer-see beh-neh	v to feel well
sentirsi male	sehn-teer-see mah-leh	v to fell ill/bad
senza	sehn-tsah	without
la sera	lah seh-rah	evening
il servizio	eel sehr-vee-tsyoh	service
il servizio lavanderia	eel sehr-vee-tsyoh lah-vahn-deh-ree-ah	laundry service
il servizio notturno	eel sehr-vee-tsyoh noht-toor-noh	all-night service
il sesto/la sesta	eel seh-stoh/lah seh-stah	sixth m/f
la settimana	lah seht-tee-mah-nah	week
il settimo/ la settima	eel seht-tee-moh/ lah seht-tee-mah	seventh m/f
lo shampoo	loh shahm-poh	shampoo

lo shopping	loh shohp-peeng	shopping
sì	see	yes adv
la sigaretta	lah see-gah-reht-tah	cigarette
la signora	lah see-nyoh-rah	Mrs.
il signore	eel see-nyoh-reh	mister
la signorina	lah see-nyoh-ree-nah	miss
simpatico/ simpatico	seem-pah-tee-koh/ seem-pah-tee-kah	nice m/f
i sintomi	ee seen-toh-mee	symptoms
il sito	eel see-toh	website
il software	eel sohft-wehr	software
la sogliola	lah soh-llyoh-lah	sole
i soldi	ee sohl-dee	money
sollevare	sohl-leh-vah-reh	v to pick up
solo	soh-loh	only adv
soltanto	sohl-tahn-toh	only adv
la sorella	lah soh-rehl-lah	sister
il souvenir	eel soo-veh-neer	souvenir
gli spaghetti	llyee spah-geht-tee	spaghetti
la Spagna	lah spah-nyah	Spain
spagnolo/spagnola	spah-nyoh-loh/spah-nyoh-lah	adj Spanish m/f
lo spagnolo	loh spah-nyoh-loh	n Spanish
la spalla	lah spahl-lah	shoulder
spedire	speh-dee-reh	v to send
spegnere	speh-nyeh-reh	v to turn off
sperare	speh-rah-reh	v to hope
spesso	spehs-soh	often adv
lo spettacolo	loh speht-tah-koh-loh	show
gli spicci	llyee spee-chee	small change
sporco/sporca	spohr-koh/spohr-kah	dirty m/f
squisito/squisita	skwee-zee-toh/skwee-zee-tah	delicious m/f
stamani	stah-mah-nee	this morning adv
la stampante	lah stahm-pahn-teh	printer
stampare	stahm-pah-reh	v to print
stanotte	stah-noht-teh	last night/tonight adv
stasera	stah-seh-rah	this evening adv
gli Stati Uniti	llyee stah-tee oo-nee-tee	United States
la statura	lah stah-too-rah	height
la stazione	lah stah-tsyoh-neh	station
le stelle	leh stehl-leh	stars
le sterline	leh stehr-lee-neh	pounds
lo stomaco	loh stoh-mah-koh	stomach
la strada	lah strah-dah	street/road
strano/strana	strah-noh/strah-nah	strange m/f
studiare	stoo-dyah-reh	v to study
lo studio medico	loh stoo-dyoh meh-dee-koh	doctor's office
subito	soo-bee-toh	immediately adv
successivo/ successiva	soo-chehs-see-voh/ soo-chehs-see-vah	following m/f
il succo d'arancia	eel sook-koh dah-rahn-chah	orange juice
il sud	eel sood	south
il supermercato	eel soo-pehr-mehr-kah-toh	supermarket
il supplemento	eel soop-pleh-mehn-toh	extra
svegliare	sveh-llyah-reh	v to wake up
svegliarsi	sveh-llyahr-see	v to wake up
la Svizzera	lah svee-tseh-rah	Switzerland
svizzero/svizzera	svee-tseh-roh/svee-tseh-rah	Swiss m/f

adj adjective	v verb	adv adverb	n noun

T

la tabaccheria	lah tah-bahk-keh-ree-ah	tobacconist's shop
la taglia	lah tah-llyah	size
tardi	tahr-dee	late adj
la tariffa intera	lah tah-reef-fah een-teh-rah	full price
il tariffario	eel tah-reef-fah-ryoh	price list
il tasso di cambio	eel tahs-soh dee kahm-byoh	exchange rate
la tastiera	lah tah-styeh-rah	keyboard
il taxi	eel tah-ksee	taxi
la tazza	lah tah-tsah	mug, cup
la tazza di caffè	lah tah-tsah dee kahf-feh	cup of coffee
il tè	eel teh	tea
il tè freddo	eel teh frehd-doh	iced tea
il teatro	eel teh-ah-troh	theatre
la tecnologia	lah tek-noh-loh-jee-ah	tecnology
tedesco/tedesca	teh-deh-skoh/teh-deh-skah	adj German m/f
il tedesco	eel teh-deh-skoh	n German
il telefonino	eel teh-leh-foh-nee-noh	cellular telephone
il telefono	eel teh-leh-foh-noh	telephone
la televisione	lah teh-leh-vee-syoh-neh	television
il televisore	eel teh-leh-vee-soh-reh	television
tempo reale	tehm-poh reh-ah-leh	real time
il terminal	eel tehr-mee-nahl	terminal
il terzo/la terza	eel tehr-tsoh/lah tehr-tsah	third m/f
la testa	lah teh-stah	head
tipico	tee-pee-koh	typical
la toilette	lah twah-leht	bathroom
la torre	lah tohr-reh	tower
la torta	lah tohr-tah	pie/cake
i tortellini	ee tohr-tehl-lee-nee	tortellini
la tosse	lah tohs-seh	n cough
il tovagliolo	eel toh-vah-llyoh-loh	napkin
il traghetto	eel trah-geht-toh	boat
il trasporto pubblico	eel trah-spohr-toh poob-blee-koh	public transportation
i travel cheque	ee trah-vehl shehk	traveler's checks m pl.
il treno	eel treh-noh	train
troppo	trohp-poh	too
troppo presto	trohp-poh preh-stoh	too early
troppo tardi	trohp-poh tahr-dee	too late
trovare	troh-vah-reh	v to find
la t-shirt	lah tee-shehrt	t-shirt
i turisti	ee too-ree-stee	tourists
tutti/tutte	toot-tee/toot-teh	all m/f
tutto/tutta	toot-toh/toot-tah	whole/all m/f

U

l'ufficio di cambio	loof-fee-choh dee kahm-byoh	currency exchange office
l'ufficio del turismo	loof-fee-choh dehl too-ree-smoh	tourism office
l'ufficio postale	loof-fee choh poh-stah-leh	post office
l'uomo	lwoh-moh	man m
uscire	oo-shee-reh	v to go out
l'uscita	loo-shee-tah	n exit/gate f

V

la vacanza	lah vah-kahn-tsah	vacation
la valigia	lah vah-lee-jyah	suitcase
le valigie	lee vah-lee-jyeh	bags/suitcases
la vasca	lah vah-skah	tub
vecchio/vecchia	vehk-kyoh/vehk-kyah	old m/f
vedere	veh-deh-reh	v to see
vegano/vegana	veh-gah-noh/veh-gah-nah	vegan m/f
vegetariano/ vegetariana	veh-jeh-tah-ryah-noh/ veh-jeh-tah-ryah-nah	vegetarian m/f
vendere	vehn-deh-reh	v to sell
venire	veh-nee-reh	v to come
verde	vehr-deh	green
verso	vehr-soh	toward
vestirsi	veh-steer-see	v to get dressed
i vestiti	ee veh-stee-tee	clothes
il vestito da donna	eel veh-stee-toh dah dohn-nah	dress
il vestito da uomo	eel veh-stee-toh dah woh-moh	suit
via internet	vyah een-tehr-neht	on the internet
viaggiare	vyah-djah-reh	v to travel
il viaggio	eel vyah-djoh	trip/journey
il viaggio di lavoro	eel vyah-djoh dee lah-voh-roh	business trip
vicino a	vee-cee-noh ah	close to adv
il vigile del fuoco	eel vee-jee-leh dehl fwoh-koh	firefighter
il vino	eel vee-noh	wine
viola	vyoh-lah	purple
visitare	vee-see-tah-reh	v to visit
il viso	eel vee-zoh	face
il visto	eel vee-stoh	visa
volentieri!	voh-lehn-tyeh-ree	with pleasure!
volere	voh-leh-reh	v to want
il volo	eel voh-loh	flight

W

il weekend	eel wee-kehnd	weekend
il wi-fi	eel wah-ee-fah-ee	wifi
la zia	lah dzee-ah	aunt
lo zio	loh-dzee-oh	uncle

Days

i giorni	ee jyohr-nee	days
lunedì	loo-neh-dee	Monday
martedì	mahr-teh-dee	Tuesday
mercoledì	mehr-koh-leh-dee	Wednesday
giovedì	jyoh-veh-dee	Thursday
venerdì	veh-nehr-dee	Friday
sabato	sah-bah-toh	Saturday
domenica	doh-meh-nee-kah	Sunday

Months

i mesi	ee may-see	months
gennaio	jeh-nah-yoh	January
febbraio	feh-brah-yoh	February
marzo	mahr-tsoh	March
aprile	ah-pree-leh	April
maggio	mah-jyoh	May
giugno	jyoo-nyoh	June
luglio	loo-llyoh	July
agosto	ah-goh-stoh	August
settembre	eh-tehm-breh	September
ottobre	oh-toh-breh	October
novembre	noh-vehm-breh	November
dicembre	dee-chehm-breh	December

adj adjective   v verb   adv adverb   n noun

Colors

 bianco/bianca
byahn-koh/byahn-kah
white m/f

 rosa
roh-zah
pink

 blu
bloo
blue

 rosso/rossa
rohs-soh/rohs-sah
red m/f

 giallo/gialla
jyah-loh/jyah-lah
yellow m/f

 verde
vayr-deh
green

 nero/nera
nay-roh/nay-rah
black m/f

viola
vyoh-lah
purple

Countries/Nationalities

 Canada — kah-nah-dah — Canada
canadese — kah-nah-deh-seh — Canadian m/f

 Irlanda — eer-lahn-dah — Ireland
irlandese — eer-lahn-deh-seh — Irish m/f

 Italia — ee-tah-lyah — Italy
italiano — ee-tah-lyah-noh — Italian m
italiana — ee-tah-lyah-nah — Italian f

 Regno Unito — reh-nyoh oo-nee-toh — United Kingdom
inglese — een-gleh-seh — English m/f

 Stati Uniti — stah-tee oo-nee-tee — United States
americano — ah-meh-ree-kah-noh — American m
americana — ah-meh-ree-kah-nah — American f

 Svizzera — svee-tseh-rah — Switzerland
svizzero — svee-tseh-roh — Swiss m
svizzera — svee-tseh-rah — Swiss f

Numbers

i numeri	ee noo-meh-ree	numbers
zero	dzeh-roh	0
uno	oo-noh	1
due	doo-eh	2
tre	treh	3
quattro	kwah-troh	4
cinque	cheen-kweh	5
sei	say	6
sette	seh-teh	7
otto	oh-toh	8
nove	noh-veh	9
dieci	dyeh-chee	10
undici	oon-dee-chee	11
dodici	doh-dee-chee	12

tredici	tray-dee-chee	13
quattordici	kwah-tohr-dee-chee	14
quindici	kween-dee-chee	15
sedici	seh-dee-chee	16
diciassette	dee-chahs-seht-teh	17
diciotto	dee-choh-toh	18
diciannove	dee-chah-noh-veh	19
venti	vehn-tee	20
trenta	trehn-tah	30
trentuno	trehn-too-noh	31
trentadue	trehn-tah-doo-eh	32
trentatré	trehn-tah-tray	33
trentaquattro	trehn-tah-kwah-troh	34
trentacinque	trehn-tah-cheen-kweh	35
trentasei	trehn-tah-say	36
trentasette	trehn-tah-seh-teh	37
trentotto	trehn-toh-toh	38
trentanove	trehn-tah-noh-veh	39
quaranta	wah-rahn-tah	40
cinquanta	cheen-kwahn-tah	50
sessanta	sehs-sahn-tah	60
settanta	seht-tahn-tah	70
settantuno	seht-tahn-too-noh	71
settantadue	seht-tahn-tah-doo-eh	72
settantatré	seht-tahn-tah-treh	73
settantaquattro	seht-tahn-tah-kwaht-troh	74
settantacinque	seht-tahn-tah-cheen-kweh	75
settantasei	seht-tahn-tah-say	76
settantasette	seht-tahn-tah-seh-teh	77
settantotto	seht-tahn-toht-toh	78
settantanove	seht-tahn-tah-noh-veh	79
ottanta	oht-tahn-tah	80
ottantuno	oht-tan-too-noh	81
ottantadue	oht-tahn-tah-doo-eh	82
novanta	noh-vahn-tah	90
novantuno	noh-vahn-too-noh	91
novantadue	noh-vahn-tah-doo-eh	92
cento	chehn-toh	100

Clothing Sizes

Women's Dresses			Men's Dress Shirts		
USA	UK	Italy	USA	UK	Italy
4	6	38	14	14	36
6	8	40	14½	14½	37
8	10	42	15	15	38
10	12	44	15½	15½	39
12	14	46	16	16	41
14	16	48	16½	16½	42
16	18	50	17	17	43

Women's Shoes			Men's Shoes		
USA	UK	Italy	USA	UK	Italy
5	2½	35	6	5½	38
6	3½	36	7	6½	39
7	4½	37	8	7½	40½
8	5½	38½	9	8½	42
9	6½	40	10	9½	43
10	7½	41	11	10½	44½
12	9½	44	12	11½	45½

| adj | adjective | v | verb | adv | adverb | n | noun |

Unit 1 Lesson 1

Activity A

1 F; 2 T; 3 F; 4 T

Activity B

Dove va in vacanza?; Vado a Napoli.; Va in aereo?; No, prendo il treno.

Lesson 2

Activity A

1 c; 2 a; 3 d; 4 b; 5 e

Activity B

1 l'aereo; 2 il traghetto; 3 la navetta; 4 l'auto; 5 la bicicletta

Lesson 3

Activity A

1 crociera; 2 taxi; 3 auto; 4 aereo

Activity B

1 Dov'è il parcheggio dei taxi?; 2 (In Italia) Noleggio un'auto.; 3 (Lei) Prende il traghetto; 4 C'è un servizio di navetta?

Lesson 4

Activity A

1 Io; 2 Lui; 3 Lei; 4 Lei

Activity B

1 Noi; 2 Loro; 3 Voi; 4 Loro

Lesson 5

Activity A

1 biglietto; 2 valigie; 3 dollari/sterline, euro; 4 passaporto; 5 auto

Activity B

Answers may vary. Possible answers:
1 fare il biglietto; 2 fare le valigie; 3 trovare un albergo; 4 prenotare un'auto a noleggio; 5 imparare meglio l'italiano

Lesson 6

Activity A

1 martedì; 2 venerdì; 3 lunedì; 4 sabato; 5 mercoledì; 6 domenica; 7 giovedì

Activity B

1 gennaio; 2 febbraio; 3 marzo; 4 aprile; 5 maggio; 6 giugno; 7 luglio; 8 agosto; 9 settembre; 10 ottobre; 11 novembre; 12 dicembre

Lesson 7

Activity A

1 check-in online; 2 numero di prenotazione; 3 stampi la Sua carta d'imbarco

Activity B

1 b; 2 d; 3 c; 4 a

Activity C

1 Click on *check-in online.*; 2 Enter your *numero di prenotazione.*; 3 Click on *scelga il posto.*; 4 Click on *stampi la Sua carta d'imbarco.*

Activity D

1 modifichi la data e l'orario del volo; 2 scelga il posto; 3 orari dei voli in tempo reale

Lesson 8

Activity A

1 Andiamo; 2 Va; 3 Vado; 4 Vanno; 5 Andate; 6 Vai; 7 Va; 8 Vanno

Activity B

1 Sì, andiamo a Genova. 2 Sì, andiamo a Bologna. 3 Sì, vanno a Cagliari. 4 Sì, vado a Venezia.

Activity C

1 Andiamo; 2 Va; 3 Vado; 4 Vanno; 5 Vai

Review

Activity A

1 il treno; 2 l'aereo; 3 la navetta; 4 l'auto

Activity B

Il sig. Conti	Dove va in vacanza?
La sig.ra Nepi	Vado a Napoli.
Il sig. Conti	Va in aereo?
La sig.ra Nepi	No, prendo il treno.

Activity C

1 lunedì; 2 martedì; 3 mercoledì; 4 giovedì; 5 venerdì; 6 sabato; 7 domenica

Activity D

io	vado
tu	vai
Lei	va
lui/lei	va
noi	andiamo
voi	andate
loro	vanno

Activity E

```
T R A G H E T T O  C I L Q S
Q N W R D Z T R A Z T Y P A
L D S C V Q L I P B N G O B
V A L I G I E W R K Z E V A
T U M O P Y I D Y M E N E T
C T P D C A Z R C V J N Y O
Z O X F E V A C A N Z A R C
V X Q T U P E P N M K I L P
V B E N C R R T Y C V O N L
A K T O M R E W R V B N M T
D Q F I G D O M E N I C A I
O T V N T R S Q H A W A T P
R C R O C I E R A R E W R T
T Q S Z D R T U I P Y O P E
```

Unit 2 Lesson 1

Activity A

1 T; 2 T; 3 F; 4 F

Activity B

Mi chiamo (your name).; Sì, sono americano/americana. No, non sono americano/americana.; Sì, sono in vacanza./No, non sono in vacanza.

Lesson 2

Activity A

1 tre; 2 due; 3 quattro; 4 cinque

Activity B

1 14.40; 2 14.05; 3 14.30; 4 13.55

Activity C

06 626 8108
071 7539172
340 5088302

Lesson 3

Activity A

1 Bene, grazie.; 2 Mi chiamo (your name).; 3 Sono (where you're from).

Activity B

1 Salve!; 2 Buongiorno.; 3 Buonasera.; 4 Buonanotte.

Lesson 4

Activity A

1 è; 2 sono; 3 siamo; 4 sono

Activity B

1 Sì, sono in vacanza./Sì, è in vacanza.; 2 Sì, Giorgio Laghi è italiano.; 3 Sì, Catherine e Julie sono americane.; 4 Sì, sono in treno.; 5 Sì, sono in taxi.

Activity C

io	sono
tu	sei
Lei	è
lui/lei	è
noi	siamo
voi	siete
loro	sono

Your Turn

Answers may vary. Possible answers: giovane, biondo/bionda, bello/bella, italiano/italiana, americano/americana, in vacanza

Lesson 5

Activity A

1 Il prossimo treno per Torino è alle 19.30.; 2 Il prossimo treno per Milano è alle 19.35.; 3 Il prossimo treno per Bologna è alle 19.50.

Activity B

1 Firenze; 2 Roma; 3 Reggio Calabria; 4 Como

Lesson 6

Activity A

1 c; 2 f; 3 d; 4 b; 5 a; 6 e

Activity B

1 il francese; il tedesco; 3 l'inglese; 4 l'italiano

Activity C

1 a; 2 c; 3 b; 4 d

Lesson 7

Activity A

Answers will vary.

Activity B

1 Vanno a sciare.; 2 È in viaggio di lavoro.; 3 Vanno a fare un'escursione.; 4 Va a Roma a studiare italiano.; 5 Sono in vacanza.

Lesson 8

Activity A

1 la valigia; 2 il treno; 3 il traghetto; 4 l'aereo

Activity B

1 a; 2 in; 3 in; 4 in; 5 a

Review

Activity A

sessantadue; undici; diciannove

Activity B

1 Sono americana e parlo inglese.; 2 Sono francese e parlo francese.; 3 Sono inglese e parlo inglese.

Activity C

1 zero sei, trentadue, cinquantaquattro, zero nove, dieci 2 zero due, ventisette, diciannove, uno quattro sei; 3 tre tre tre, diciassette, quarantanove, due uno cinque

Activity D

1 10.15; 2 12.20; 3 14.45; 21.50

Activity E

1 il; 2 l'; 3 la; 4 il; 5 l'

Challenge

Answers may vary. Possible answers: 1 L'Italia, italiano/a, l'italiano; 2 Gli Stati Uniti. americano/americana, l'inglese; 3 L'Inghilterra, inglese, l'inglese; 4 La Francia, francese, il francese; 5 La Germania, tedesco/tedesca, il tedesco

Unit 3 Lesson 1

Activity A

Cognome: Corsini; Nome: Marina; Cittadinanza: italiana; Data di nascita: 5 marzo 1975; Data del volo: 23 marzo 2010; Volo: 2083

Activity B

1 b; 2 d; 3 a; 4 e; 5 c

Lesson 2

Activity A

1 a; 2 e; 3 b; 4 c; 5 d

Activity B

1 arrivare al terminal; 2 passare il controllo passaporti; 3 andare al ritiro bagagli; 4 passare la dogana; 5 trovare l'uscita

Activity C

		¹C		²V		³R	
	⁴A	R	R	I	V	I
		R		S		T
		R		T		I
⁵A	E	R	E	O		R
		L				O
		L				
		O				

Lesson 3

Activity A

1 b; 2 a; 3 a; 4 b

Activity B

1 questo; 2 questi; 3 questa; 4 queste

Lesson 4

Activity A

1 Abbiamo; 2 Ho; 3 ha; 4 hanno

Activity B

io	ho
tu	hai
Lei	ha
lui/lei	ha
noi	abbiamo
voi	avete
loro	hanno

Activity C

1 c; 2 b; 3 e; 4 a; 5 d

Lesson 5

Activity A

1 F; 2 T; 3 F; 4 T

Activity B

Andiamo all'Hotel Mercurio.; via Fontana 25. Posso pagare con la carta di credito?; Mi può dare la ricevuta, per favore?

Activity C

1 Sa l'indirizzo?; 2 Mi dispiace.; 3 Posso accettare soltanto contanti.

Lesson 6

Activity A

1 a; 2 a; 3 b

Activity B

1 Selezionare "biglietto singolo"; 2 Introdurre monete, banconote o carta di credito; 3 Confermare; 4 Ritirare biglietti

Lesson 7

Activity A

Stazione Battistini

Activity B

1 Stazione Termini; 2 Stazione Colli Albani

Lesson 8

Activity A

1 la; 2 l'; 3 il

Activity B

1 una; 2 un; 3 un'

Activity A

1 un; 2 la; 3 un'; 4 il

Review

Activity A

Cognome (your last name [surname]); Nome (your first name); Cittadinanza (your nationality); Data di nascita (your birth date); Luogo di nascita (your place of birth)

Activity B

1 Mi può dare la ricevuta, per favore?; 2 Posso pagare con la carta di credito?; 3 Sa l'indirizzo?

Challenge

Answers may vary. Possible answers:; 1 Ho fame.; 2 Ho sete.; 3 Ho sonno.; 4 Ho caldo.; 5 Ho paura.

Activity C

1 una valigia; 2 un passaporto; 3 un'auto

Activity D

1 Prenda la linea B direzione Laurentina. Scenda a Termini. Prenda la linea A, direzione Anagnina. Scenda alla settima fermata.; 2 Prenda la linea A, direzione Anagnina. Scenda a Termini. Prenda la linea B direzione Laurentina. Scenda al capolinea.

Unit 4 Lesson 1

Activity A

1 sette notti; 2 due persone; 3 novanta euro

Activity B

1 hotel; 2 none; 3 doppia; 4 euro

Activity C

1 Buongiorno. Ho una prenotazione a nome di (your name).;
2. Quanto costa a notte?

Lesson 2

Activity A 1 T; 2 F; 3 T; 4 T; 5 F

Activity B 1 c; 2 d; 3 a; 4 b

Lesson 3

Activity A

1 Ho bisogno di un letto supplementare.; 2 Ho prenotato via Internet.; Avete una camera per non fumatori?

Activity B

1 Quanto costa a notte?; 2 Avete una camera per non fumatori?; 3 Avete una camera con l'aria condizionata?; 4 Avete una camera doppia?

Lesson 4

Activity A

1 La camera non è al piano terra.; 2 Nella camera non c'è il bagno.; 3 La doccia non funziona.; 4 Non ho bisogno di un lettino.

Activity B

1 No, Harry non è italiano.; 2 No, il telefono non funziona.; 3 No, non c'è la doccia.; 4 No, Peter non parla italiano.

Lesson 5

Activity A

1 No, il letto è grande.; 2 Sì, c'è un televisore; 3 Sì, ci sono una sedia e una scrivania.

Activity B 1 Il mio; 2 La loro; 3 Il suo; 4 Le vostre

Lesson 6

Activity A la scala

Activity B

1 asciugamani; 2 carta igienica; 3 shampoo; 4 saponetta

Activity C

Answers may vary. Possible answers:
la camera: la coperta, le lenzuola, il cuscino, il bollitore
il bagno: l'asciugamano, la saponetta, la doccia, lo shampoo

Lesson 7

Activity A

1 Mi può svegliare alle 7?; 2 Mi può chiamare un taxi?; 3 A che ora devo lasciare la camera?; 4 Mi può rifare la camera?

Activity B

1 b; 2 a; 3 d; 4 c

Lesson 8

Activity A

io	parlo
tu	parli
Lei	parla
lui/lei	parla
noi	parliamo
voi	parlate
loro	parlano

Activity B

1 parlano; 2 Visitiamo; 3 Studio; 4 resta; 5 Cerca

Activity C

1 c; 2 d; 3 a; 4 e; 5 d

Review

Activity A

1 il letto; 2 il fon; 3 gli asciugamani; 4 la doccia

Activity B

1 Lei non studia spagnolo.
2 Il ferro da stiro non funziona.
3 Non visitiamo il Vaticano.
4 Le nostre camere non sono piccole.

Activity C

1 il mio telefono; 2 la sua camera; 3 le loro coperte; 4 la tua/Sua chiave

Activity D

```
D R T P P C S A M G S L S B G
C O M O D A W Q X A I M K L P
F Z Q M K L S A P O N E T T A
S D J L P F C B E S G D S E S
K Y P G T V R K D C O C C L X
P N I E E S I R C Z L Z R E Z
O M C H I A V E A A O S U V X
W O C Q C V A D V C D T T I V
V L O A V I N F K A K E E S G
Z I L Z O T I W Y M P I D O L
P I A N O E A S C E N S O R E
M U P T M Z P C G R U E V E T
Y N R U S V C U V A H D X D T
P V A S C A R I C D V I A B O
Q G T O Z X D O P P I A Q N T
```

Challenge

domando; domandi; domanda; domanda; domandiamo; domandate; domandano
ballo; balli; balla; balla; balliamo; ballate; ballano
lavoro; lavori; lavora; lavora; lavoriamo; lavorate; lavorano
amo; ami; ama; ama; amiamo; amate; amano

Unit 5 Lesson 1

Activity A 1 T; 2 F; 3 T; 4 F

Activity B

Anna	Che facciamo oggi?
Francesco	Prima dobbiamo andare in banca.
Anna	Dopo possiamo andare a visitare il Colosseo?
Francesco	Sì! Io vorrei visitare anche una chiesa.
Anna	A Roma c'è sempre molto da fare!

Lesson 2

Activity A 1 la chiesa; 2 l'Ufficio Postale; 3 la banca; 4 il castello

Activity B 1 l'ufficio del turismo; 2 il mercato; 3 il parco; 4 il museo

Activity C 1 d; 2 c; 3 a; 4 b; 5 f; 6 e

Your Turn

Answers may vary. Possible answers:
1 il castello; 2 i monumento; 3 il museo; 4 la piazza

Lesson 3

Activity A 1 dollari/euro; 2 sterline/dollari; 3 euro/sterline

Activity B 3; 1; 4; 2

Activity C

1 Il bancomat mi ha preso la carta.; 2 A che ora apre la banca?;
3 Vorrei cambiare dei travel cheque in euro.; 4 Dov'è il bancomat più
vicino?; 5 Qual è il tasso di cambio?; 6 A che ora chiude la banca?

Your Turn

Answers may vary. Possible answers:
Vorrei cambiare dei dollari in euro.; Vorrei cambiare delle sterline
in euro.

Lesson 4

Activity A

1. Vedo il castello. 2. Vede il mercato. 3. Vediamo il ponte.
4. Vedete la piazza.

Activity B

io	posso
tu	puoi
Lei	può
lui/lei	può
noi	possiamo
voi	potete
loro	possono

Activity C

1. Possiamo andare prima al Colosseo. 2. Vede la fermata
dell'autobus? 3. Può prendere il 14 e scendere in via di Ripetta.
4. Non vedo nessun bancomat.

Activity D

1 Sì, posso/può andare in vacanza.; 2 Sì, può visitare il museo.;
3 Sì, possiamo visitare il Comune.; 4 Sì, vedo un bancomat.; 5 Sì,
l'ufficio di cambio può cambiare di dollari in euro.; 6 Sì, puoi/
può andare in banca.

Lesson 5

Activity A

1 Giri a sinistra.; 2 Vada sempre dritto.; 3 Giri a destra.; 4 Prenda
la seconda a sinistra.

Activity B 1 Fontana di Trevi; 2 Palazzo Chigi

Lesson 6

Activity A

1 diciotto centesimi; 2 tre euro
e settanta centesimi; 3 trenta-
cinque euro; 4 venti euro

Activity B

1 millecinquecento euro e ses-
santa; 2 novantanove euro e
novantanove; 3 settantacinque
centesimi

Lesson 7

Activity A 1 d; 2 a; 3 b; 4 c

Activity B

1 Per favore, potrebbe ripetere?; 2 Che significa?; 3 Mi sono
persa.; 4 Mi dispiace, ma non ho capito.; 5 Per favore, potrebbe
indicarlo sulla cartina?; 6 Mi scusi, cerco la banca.; 7 Per favore,
potrebbe parlare più lentamente?; 8 Per favore, potrebbe indi-
carmi la strada?

Lesson 8

Activity A 1 quando; 2 chi; 3 quanto; 4 dove

Activity B 1 Quanto; 2 Come; 3 Dov'; 4 Chi

Activity C 1 e; 2 d; 3 f; 4 b; 5 c; 6 a

Activity D

Review

Activity A 1 il ponte; 2 il museo; 3 la chiesa; 4 il castello

Activity B 1 Possiamo; 2 Potete; 3 Posso; 4 Possono

Activity C

io	vedo
tu	vedi
Lei	vede
lui/lei	vede
noi	vediamo
voi	vedete
loro	vedono

Activity D

1 Potrebbe parlare più lentamente?; 2 Potrebbe scriverlo?;
3 Quanto costa?; 4 Dov'è la chiesa?

Activity E 1 d; 2 a; 3 g; 4 b; 5 f; 6 e; 7 c

Challenge

1 seicentonovantadue; 2 mille trecento novantanove; 3 duemila
dieci; 4 settantasette

Unit 6 Lesson 1

Activity A

1 un ristorante; 2 italiana; 3 di fronte alla

Activity B

1 No, a Edward piace tutta la cucina italiana.; 2 Sì, c'è una pizzeria accanto all'Ufficio Postale. 3 No, l'Ufficio Postale è di fronte alla chiesa.

Activity C

1 b; 2 d; 3 e; 4 a; 5 c

Lesson 2

Activity A

1 la torta; 2 il formaggio; 3 il pane; 4 l'insalata; 5 la bistecca

Activity B

Answers will vary.

Lesson 3

Activity A

1 la forchetta; 2 il cucchiaio; 3 il coltello; 4 il bicchiere

Activity B

1 un bicchiere; 2 una forchetta; 3 un tovagliolo

Activity C

1 Sono vegetariano/vegetariana.; 2 Mi può portare il conto?; 3 Dov'è la toilette?; 4 Io prendo l'insalata.

Your Turn

Answers will vary. Possible answers:
Io prendo l'agnello e l'insalata.; Io prendo il pollo.; Io prendo un bicchiere d'acqua.

Lesson 4

Activity A

1 prendono; 2 Prendi; 3 Prendo; 4 Prendiamo; 5 Prendete

Activity B

1 Carlo prende l'insalata.; 2 Noi prendiamo la minestra.; 3 Voi prendete i gamberetti.; 4 Loro prendono le cozze.

Activity C

1. Un vegetariano prende l'insalata.; 2. Per andare in Italia prendo l'aereo.; 3. Con la carne gli italiani prendono un contorno.; 4. Prendiamo un gelato come dessert.

Lesson 5

Activity A

Cristina: a, b, e; Martino: c, d, e

Activity B

1 Prendo il menù del giorno.; 2 Come dessert prendo un gelato.; 3 Prendo la bistecca ben cotta.; 4 Prendo una bottiglia di vino.

Lesson 6

Activity A

1 Emma prende una Coca-Cola.; 2 Carla e Michela prendono un caffè.; 3 Noi prendiamo una bottiglia di vino.

Activity B

Activity C

Answers may vary.
Possible answers:
la colazione: il caffè, il cappuccino, il tè, il latte, il succo d'arancia
il pranzo: l'acqua, il vino bianco, il vino rosso, la Coca-Cola
la cena: l'acqua, il vino bianco, il vino rosso, la birra

Activity D

1 b; 2 f; 3 a; 4 e; 5 d; 6 c

Lesson 7

Activity A

1 Che cosa desidera?; 2 Buon appetito!; 3 A Lei!; 4 Desidera altro?

Activity B

1 acqua naturale; 2 un aperitivo; 3 acqua gassata; 4 un digestivo

Activity C

Answer may vary. Possible answers:
Prendo il pollo, un'insalata e un gelato.; Un caffè, grazie.

Lesson 8

Activity A

io	voglio
tu	vuoi
Lei	vuole
lui/lei	vuole
noi	vogliamo
voi	volete
loro	vogliono

Activity B

io	bevo
tu	bevi
Lei	beve
lui/lei	beve
noi	beviamo
voi	bevete
loro	bevono

Activity C 1 vuole; 2 voglio; 3 vogliono; 4 vogliamo

Activity D 1 beve; 2 Bevi; 3 Beve; 4 Bevono

Review

Activity A

1 Mi può portare il conto?; 2 Prendo il pollo.; 3 Bevo un caffè.; 4 Dov'è la toilette?

Activity B 1 il pane; 2 il caffè; 3 il dolce; 4 il succo d'arancia

Activity C 1 il coltello; 2 la sogliola; 3 un digestivo

Activity D

1 formaggio; 2 pane; 3 torta; 4 gelato; 5 sogliola
Bonus word: pasta

Activity E

1 vuole; 2 Beviamo; 3 Prende; 4 Vogliono; 5 bevo; 6 Prendi

Challenge

prendo; prendi; prende; prende; prendiamo; prendete; prendono
voglio; vuoi; vuole; vuole; vogliamo; volete; vogliono
bevo; bevi; beve; beve; beviamo; bevete; bevono

Unit 7 Lesson 1

Activity A

1 La Pietà; 2 la t-shirt Roma; 3 il libro sull'Italia; 4 la tazza

Activity B 1 sì; 2 no; 3 no; 4 sì

Activity C

Answers may vary. Possible answers:
1 la t-shirt Roma; 2 la Torre Pendente in miniatura; 3 il portachiavi Colosseo; 4 il libro sull'Italia

Lesson 2

Activity A

1 il negozio di scarpe; 2 la gioielleria; 3 la panetteria; 4 la libreria

Activity B

1 il centro commerciale; 2 il negozio di scarpe; 3 la libreria; 4 la profumeria

Activity C 1 b; 2 d; 3 e; 4 a; 5 c

Lesson 3

Activity A 1 d; 2 a; 3 b; 4 c

Activity B

1 Mi può fare uno sconto?; 2 Ci devo pensare.; 3 Volevo solo dare un'occhiata.; 4 Ho soltanto 20 euro.

Lesson 4

Activity A

parto; parti; parte; parte; partiamo; partite; partono

Activity B 1 scende; 2 Rispondiamo; 3 Finite; 4 Partono

Activity C 1 c; 2 a; 3 b; 4 d

Lesson 5

Activity A c (la camicia, il cappotto, la cravatta)

Activity B

Answers may vary. Possible answers:
1 i jeans, il cappotto; 2 i pantaloni, la camicia, la cravatta; 3 il giubbino, la cintura

Activity C 204€

Activity D

```
R F C S C B H J Y D M K O P R P V X C C R A V A T T A A F G
C S S X V N J V D R M L O C M A C S H K L N G F D C G R I
M R W A D G C E N J F I D X K L F N S J T D X M U O M O M U
S O D S B J K S B D S F H M X N K O T H K V N C C S X N J B
S Z D H U R U T S Z B J K L I Y R C X A C S G H K Y O P L B
A E F A E G Y I L I Y R D X W N K Y F S L T D Z V T W Q Z I
Z Q D C Q Z Q T E R G Y U F C Z V G Y H J O S B H U I I K N
T C S X R V B O D R S Z W A Q E Z D T N J K N P L J G X O
A D A H F T E T U H F D O N N A T D S F H M B I S C G U I K
Q G Z P G N K U K L H Y T R D X V G F S A B H J K O L J U F
A B F Z P J I T K L T F D B O R S A S E W H N M K T E E W A
D G J A X O K Y I E S Z U O P R W Q V B N K L O T P W A D F
S B G T P A T H J L U H T F R E D A W C V B N M G H Y N W Q
S L O U O C P T E T F V B N C I N T U R A W S F G B H S J K
W A V G B N B K O U T E T H J K K L Y E W V N K L T E Q A F
```

Lesson 6

Activity A

1 gioiello; 2 giocattolo; 3 cosmetici; 4 cartolina

Activity B

3; 1; 2

Activity C

1 c; 2 d; 3 a; 4 b

Activity D

Answers may vary. Possible answers:
un gioiello; un profumo; dei cosmetici; una scatola di cioccolatini; un disegno

Lesson 7

Activity A

1 c; 2 a; 3 b

Activity B

1 b; 2 b; 3 a

Lesson 8

Activity A

1 bel; 2 cari; 3 grande; 4 brutta

Activity B

1 un maglione verde; 2 dei jeans neri; 3 una camicia grigia; 4 una cintura blu

Review

Activity A

1 il mercato; 2 il centro commerciale; 3 il negozio di vestiti; 4 la libreria

Activity B

1 Quanto costa?; 2 Lo può incartare?; 3 Mi può fare uno sconto ?; 4 Dov'è la cassa?

Challenge

1 visito; visiti; visita; visita; visitiamo; visitate; visitano
2 chiedo; chiedi; chiede; chiede; chiediamo; chiedete; chiedono
3 capisco; capisci; capisce; capiamo; capite; capiscono

Activity C

1 b; 2 b; 3 a; 4 a

Activity D

Drawings will vary.
1 a small black car; 2 a large bottle of red wine; 3 a beautiful blue handbag

Unit 8 Lesson 1

Activity A

1 a; 2 b; 3 a; 4 a

Activity B

Robert Mi scusi, c'è un Internet Point qui vicino? Vorrei controllare la posta.
Portiere Sì, c'è un Internet Point qui di fronte. Ma Lei ha un portatile?
Robert Sì.
Portiere Allora vada al bar in fondo alla strada: c'è il Wi-Fi gratuito.
Robert Grazie mille!

Activity C

1 Vuole controllare la posta.; 2 Sì, c'è un Internet Point di fronte all'albergo.; C'è il Wi-Fi gratuito.

Lesson 2

Activity A

1 a; 2 b; 3 a

Activity B

1 il mouse; 2 la stampante; 3 lo schermo; 4 la tastiera; 5 Internet

Activity C

1 il cellulare; il portatile; 3 l'adattatore; 4 la chiavetta USB

Lesson 3

Activity A

1 Ci sono hot-spot gratuiti?; 2 Quanto costa collegarsi per 10 minuti?; 3 Devo mandare un'e-mail.

Activity B

1 Quanto costa collegarsi per 30 minuti/mezz'ora?; 2 C'è il Wi-Fi in albergo?; 3 Posso stampare la carta d'imbarco?; 4 Ci sono hotspot gratuiti?

Lesson 4

Activity A

1 fa; 2 Fai; 3 Fate; 4 fa; 5 Faccio; 6 Facciamo; 7 fanno

Activity B

1 a; 2 b; 3 a; 4 a

Activity C

1 Fa bel tempo.; 2 Fa freddo.; 3 Fa caldo.; 4 Fa brutto tempo.

Lesson 5

Activity A

1 T; 2 F; 3 F; 4 T

Activity B

1 Sollevare la cornetta; 2 Introdurre la carta o digitare il numero verde; 3 Digitare il numero; 4 Riagganciare; 5 Ritirare la carta

Activity C

1 a; 2 b; 3 b; 4 b

Lesson 6

Activity A

1 cliccare; 2 scrivere; 3 stampare; 4 accendere

Activity B

Activity C 1 a; 2 a; 3 a; 4 a

Lesson 7

Activity A 1 c; 2 a; 3 b

Activity B Sono Sandro.; Posso parlare con Elena?

Activity C

1 Sono (your name).; 2 Ha sbagliato numero.; 3 Pronto?; 4 Gli/Le dica di richiamarmi, per favore.

Lesson 8

Activity A scrivo; scrivi; dice; scriviamo; leggete; dicono

Activity B

1 Sì, scrivo ai miei amici.; 2 Sì, leggo spesso le e-mail.; 3 Dico "Pronto?"

Activity C 1. Giorgio legge.; 2. Lucia scrive.; 3 Fabio dice "Pronto?"

Review

Activity A

1 C'è un Internet Point vicino all'albergo?; 2 Posso mandare un'e-mail?; 3 Posso stampare la carta d'imbarco?; 4 Posso parlare con (name)?

Activity B

io	scrivo	leggo
tu	scrivi	leggi
Lei	scrive	legge
lui/lei	scrive	legge
noi	scriviamo	leggiamo
voi	scrivete	leggete
loro	scrivono	leggono

Activity C 1 d; 2 a; 3 b; 4 e; 5 c; 6 g; 7 f

Activity D

1 Fanno una passeggiata.; 2 Fa caldo.; 3. Facciamo la fila.; 4 Faccio le valigie.

Challenge

Answers will vary. Possible answer:
A: Pronto?
B: Buongiorno, sono (your name). Posso parlare con (name)?
A: (Name) non c'è. Vuole lasciare un messaggio?
B: Gli/Le dica di richiamarmi, per favore.

Unit 9 Lesson 1

Activity A

1 Nadia vuole uscire.; 2 Vuole andare in discoteca.; 3 No, Alessio non può fare molto tardi.

Activity B Voglio uscire!; A ballare.; No, non posso fare molto tardi.

Lesson 2

Activity A 1 a; 2 b; 3 a; 4 a

Activity B

Answers may vary. Possible answers:
1 il bar; 2 il cinema; 3 il concerto

Activity C 1 teatro; 2 concerto; 3 cinema; 4 discoteca; 5 bar

Activity D 1 il Casinò; 2 il cinema; 3 il bar; 4 la discoteca

Lesson 3

Activity A

1 A Renata piace la musica classica.; 2 A Chiara e Alfredo piace la musica pop.; 3 A me piace il jazz.

Activity B 1 dura; 2 costa; 3 consigliare

Activity C

Quanto costa il biglietto?; Quanto (tempo) dura il concerto?; A che ora finisce il concerto?

Lesson 4

Activity A 1 a; 2 a; 3 b

Activity B 1 al; 2 dal; 3 a; 4 dalla

Activity C

Answers may vary. Possible answers:
1 Voglio andare al cinema.; 2 Voglio andare al bingo.; 3 Voglio andare in discoteca.

Activity D 1 al; 2 dalla; 3 alle; 4 dai; 5 alla; 6 dagli

Lesson 5

Activity A

1 Concerto Rock; 2 Serata hip-hop; 3 *Sei personaggi in cerca d'autore*; Total: 50€

Activity B

Answers may vary. Possible answers:
1 Concerto jazz; 2 Vivaldi, *Le quattro stagioni*; 3 Serata hip-hop

Activity C 1 b; 2 a; 3 a

Lesson 6

Activity A 1 la pista da ballo; 2 il bar; 3 il guardaroba

Activity B 1 il buttafuori; 2 il DJ; 3 la barman

Activity C 1 b; 2 a; 3 a; 4 a; 5 a

Lesson 7

Activity A

Answers may vary. Possible answers:
1 Le posso offrire un drink?; 2 Le va di ballare?; 3 Di che cosa si occupa?

Activity B

1 È libero?; 2 Mi posso sedere?; 3 Disturbo?; 4 Le posso offrire un drink?

Activity C

1 È libero?; 2 Di che cosa si occupa?; 3 Le va di ballare?; 4 Mi posso sedere?

Lesson 8

Activity A

1 Venite; 2 vengo; 3 Vieni; 4 Vengono; 5 Vieni; 6 Viene; 7 Viene

Activity B

1 esci; 2 Escono; 3 esce; 4 usciamo; 5 Esco; 6 Usciamo; 7 Esce

Activity C

Answers may vary. Possible answers:
1 Usciamo con (name).; 2 Vengono alle (time).; 3 Sì, esco con voi.; 4 No, Marina non viene.

Activity D 1 a; 2 b; 3 a; 4 a

Review

Activity A

Answers may vary. Possible answers:
1 la discoteca; 2 il concerto; 3 il teatro

Activity B 1 a; 2 b; 3 a

Activity C

Activity D 1 a; 2 a; 3 b

Activity E

io	esco	vengo
tu	esci	vieni
Lei	esce	viene
lui/lei	esce	viene
noi	usciamo	veniamo
voi	uscite	venite
loro	escono	vengono

Challenge esco; esci; esce; esce; usciamo; uscite; escono

Unit 10 Lesson 1

Activity A 1 T; 2 T; 3 T; 4 F

Activity B

Cerco la farmacia notturna.; Mi può indicare la strada?; Grazie mille!

Lesson 2

Activity A

1 i vigili del fuoco (18); 2 il pronto soccorso (118); 3 la polizia (113)/i Carabinieri (112)

Activity B

1 il vigile del fuoco; 2 il medico; 3 il poliziotto; 4 l'infermiera

Activity C

1 la farmacia; 2 lo studio medico; 3 l'ospedale

Lesson 3

Activity A

1 Al ladro!; 2 Al fuoco!; 3 Aiuto!; 4 Attenzione!; 5 Mi sono rotto/rotta la gamba.; 6 Sono diabetico/diabetica.

Activity B

1 Mi sono rotta il braccio.; 2 Sono malata.; 3 Mi sono rotto la gamba.; 4 Sono asmatica.

Activity C

1 aiuto; 2 al fuoco; 3 attenzione; 4 al ladro

Activity D 1 c; 2 a; 3 d; 4 b

Lesson 4

Activity A 1 si; 2 ci; 3 ti; 4 Si

Activity B

1 Giorgio si lava i denti.; 2 Anna si fa la doccia.; 3 Lui si chiama Paolo.

Activity C 1 e; 2 a; 3 c; 4 f; 5 b; 6 d

Lesson 5

Activity A 1 T; 2 T; 3 T; 4 F

Activity B

Ha la tosse.; Ha mal di testa.; Ha la febbre.; Ha mal di gola.

Activity C

1 Ho mal di testa.; 2 Non mi sento bene.; 3 Ho l'influenza.; 4 Mi fa male la gola.

Your Turn

Answers may vary. Possible answers:
Non mi sento bene. Ho mal di testa/Mi fa male la testa. Ho la tosse e mi fa male la gola/ho mal di gola. Ho l'influenza.

Lesson 6

Activity A

1 l'occhio; 2 il naso; 3 l'orecchio; 4 la lingua

Activity B

1 il piede; 2 il braccio; 3 il petto; 4 la mano

Activity C

Answers may vary. Possible answers:
il corpo: il braccio; la gamba; il ginocchio; il piede; la testa
il viso: la bocca; la lingua; gli occhi; l'orecchio; il naso

Lesson 7

Activity A

pasticche per la tosse; cerotti; antiacido; aspirina

Activity B

1 delle pasticche per la gola; 2 una confezione di aspirina; 3 uno sciroppo per la tosse

Activity C

1 Che cosa mi consiglia per la nausea?; 2 Che cosa mi consiglia per il raffreddore?; 3 Che cosa mi consiglia per il mal d'auto?

Lesson 8

Activity A

mangiare	mangiato
riuscire	riuscito
vendere	venduto
bere	bevuto
rispondere	risposto
viaggiare	viaggiato
scrivere	scritto
fare	fatto
pagare	pagato

Activity B

Answers may vary. Possible answers:
1 Sì, ho visto il Colosseo./No, non ho visto il Colosseo.; 2 Sì, ho scelto la pizza./No, non ho scelto la pizza.; 3 Sì, ho risposto al telefono./No, non ho risposto al telefono.; 4 Sì, ho comprato un vestito./No, non ho comprato un vestito.; 5 Sì, ho fatto le valigie. No, non ho fatto le valigie.

Review

Activity A

1 Al ladro!; 2 Aiuto!; 3 Mi sono rotto/rotta la gamba.; 4 Mi fanno male i piedi.; 5 Mi fa male la gola./Ho mal di gola.

Activity B

1 Massimo è malato.; 2 Lucia ha mal di schiena.; 3 Matteo si veste.; 4 Alice si lava i denti.

Activity C

Mi fa male la testa.; Ho la febbre.; Ho mal di gola.; Ho la tosse.

Activity D

1 Ho viaggiato con la mia famiglia.; 2 Abbiamo scelto un primo e un secondo.; 3 Anna e Luisa hanno mangiato un gelato.; 4 Giorgio non ha risposto al cellulare.; 5 Hai guardato la televisione.

Challenge

Answers may vary. Possible answers:
il braccio, la testa, gli occhi, il naso, la gamba, l'orecchio, la mano, il piede, la lingua, il ginocchio

Unit 11 Lesson 1

Activity A

1 ci sono; 2 diverto; 3 visitato; 4 buoni ristoranti; 5 ho parlato

Activity B

visitare il Colosseo; parlare con le persone; mangiare molto

Activity C

Answers may vary. Possible answer:
Roma è una bella città. A Roma mi diverto. Ci sono molte cose da
fare. Ho visitato il Colosseo, la Fontana di Trevi e il Vaticano. Ci
sono molti ristoranti e io ho mangiato molto.
A presto!
(your name)

Lesson 2

Activity A 1 a; 2 a; 3 b; 4 a

Activity B

Answers may vary. Possible answers:
1 dei vestiti; 2 dei giocattoli; 3 una camicia; 4 un quadro; 5 un libro

Lesson 3

Activity A

1 Rimaniamo in contatto.; 2 Mi sono divertito/divertita.; 3 Mi
mancherai.; 4 A presto, spero!; 5 È stato un piacere.

Activity B

1 presto; 2 prossima; 3 piacere; 4 divertito; 5 contatto
Bonus word: padre

Activity C 1 Alla prossima!; 2 È stato un piacere.; 3 Mi mancherai.

Lesson 4

Activity A

Answers may vary. Possible answers:
1 Mio padre è più anziano di mia madre.; 2 L'italiano è più bello
dell'inglese.; 3 Il dolce è più caro dell'insalata.; 4 Il vino è buono
come la birra.; 5 Mia nonna è più alta di mia madre.

Activity B 1 più; 2 come; 3 meno

Activity C 1 più; 2 meno; 3 più; 4 meno; 5 migliore

Lesson 5

Activity A 1 T; 2 F; 3 T; 4 T

Activity B

Sì, ho fatto le valigie.; Sì, la città mi è piaciuta (molto).; Sì, ho
visitato molti monumenti.; Anche per me!

Activity C

1 Sì, Ryan ha fatto le valigie.; 2 Sì, a Ryan la città è piaciuta
molto.; 3 Sì, Ryan ha visitato molti monumenti.; 4 Sì, Ryan ha
comprato molti souvenir.

Lesson 6

Activity A

Answers may vary. Possible answers:
1 Il viaggio è interessante.; 2 La cena era squisita.; 3 La città è
magnifica.; 4 I monumenti sono incredibili.; 5 L'albergo è orribile.

Activity B

1 interessante; 2 noioso; 3 romantica; 4 orribili; 5 magnifico

Activity C

buoni: squisito; simpatico; interessante; magnifico
cattivi: orribile; noioso; pessimo; strano

Your Turn Answers will vary.

Lesson 7

Activity A

1 Sono rimasto/rimasta 6 giorni.; 2 Sono andato/andata in Italia.;
3 Non vedo l'ora di vedere le foto.; 4 Non vedo l'ora di rientrare.

Activity B 1 a; 2 b; 3 a

Activity C

Answers may vary. Possible answers:
1 Sì, sono andato/andata in Italia.; 2 Sì, ho conosciuto molte
persone.; 3 Sì, sono stati tutti molto gentili.

Lesson 8

Activity A

1 Sono rimaste tre giorni a Pisa.; 2 È arrivata alle 3 di notte.; 3 Si
è divertito.; 4 Sono venuto con la mia famiglia.; 5 Siamo andate
all'aeroporto.

Activity B 1 è; 2 sono; 3 ha; 4 abbiamo; 5 siete

Activity C

venire	venuto
andare	andato
rimanere	rimasto
arrivare	arrivato
uscire	uscito
nascere	nato
passare	passato
scendere	sceso
cadere	caduto

Review

Activity A

Answers will vary. Possible answer:
Sono andato in Italia. Mi sono divertito. Gli italiani sono molto
simpatici. I ristoranti sono molto buoni e io ho mangiato molto.
Non vedo l'ora di ritornare!
A presto!
Brian

Activity B 1 più alto; 2 meno bella/più brutta; 3 malato

Activity C 1 b; 2 b; 3 b; 4 b

Activity D

Answers may vary. Possible answers:
1 Sì, mi sono divertito/divertita.; 2 Sono andato/andata in Italia.;
3 Sono arrivato/arrivata il 5 luglio.; 4 Sono rimasto/rimasta due
settimane.; 5 Sono rientrato/rientrata il 19 luglio.

Challenge

Answers may vary. Possible answers:
andare, venire, arrivare, salire, scendere, partire, ritornare, rientrare, uscire, nascere